With Compliments

[handwritten signature]

SENSITIVITY TRAINING FOR EDUCATORS: AN EVALUATION

SENSITIVITY TRAINING FOR EDUCATORS: AN EVALUATION

by
J. L. Khanna, Ph.D.

Professor, Department of Psychiatry
University of Tennessee Center for
the Health Sciences, Memphis, Tennessee

and
Prabha Khanna, Ph.D.

Professor, Department of Psychology
Memphis State University
Memphis, Tennessee

VANTAGE PRESS
New York / Washington / Atlanta
Los Angeles / Chicago

FIRST EDITION

Copyright © 1980 by
J. L. Khanna, Ph.D. and Prabha Khanna, Ph.D.

Published by Vantage Press, Inc.
516 West 34th Street, New York, New York 10001

Manufactured in the United States of America
Standard Book Number 533-04031-0

Library of Congress Catalog Card No.: 78-64688

To
Kanwal and Mukti

CONTENTS

PREFACE

This book describes the evaluation of a three-year sensitivity training program for educators of the Upper Cumberland region in Tennessee. The program was funded by Project Upper Cumberland, Title III, ESEA.

Chapter I discusses the special subculture represented by the sample.

Chapter II gives a brief overview of the assessment program. The assessment used internal and external criteria and matched control groups to study the effects of sensitivity training. Internal criteria represented those changes that occurred within a person. These are discussed in Chapter III.

External criteria were defined as variables that are part of a person's environment. This part of the assessment is discussed in Chapter IV.

Chapter V describes the assessment of the third-year participants. It involved open-ended interviews of the subjects in the control and the experimental groups.

Chapter VI summarizes the main findings of the evaluation and some of the limitations of the study.

Any large evaluation program cannot be completed without the help of numerous persons who are directly or indirectly related to the program. It is impossible for us, within the confines of these pages, to thank everyone who was of invaluable help.

Keeping these limitations in mind, we would like to express our sincere appreciation to the following without whose help this research would not have been possible: to Dr. O. C. Stewart for encouraging scientific research in this area and for his constant advice and help with the problems that came up in this investigation; to Dr. Edell Hearne for arranging the subjects for the control group and administering the tests to them; to Dr. Douglas Norman for his overall help and encouragement in providing the facilities that made this work possible and, also, for arranging subjects and administering tests to them in the interest of this evaluation; to Dr. Jerry Wesch for his invaluable help as a research assistant, especially in the regression analysis; to Mr. Harold Williams and Mrs. Muriel Davis for their help in collection of the data; to Dr. R. L. Frye for his invaluable help in the factor analysis of some of the data; to Dr. Herbert Eber for his invaluable help as a research consultant, especially with regard to the M.A.T. analysis; and to Mrs. Carla Ryan and Mr. Kanwal Khanna for the arduous task of typing and proofreading the manuscript.

J. L. Khanna
Prabha Khanna

SENSITIVITY TRAINING
FOR EDUCATORS:
AN EVALUATION

Chapter I

INTRODUCTION

Foothills west of the better-known Smoky Mountains and a river's headwaters give the Upper Cumberlands of Tennessee their name. The region is one of timber, small farms, isolated rural communities built around schools and churches, and county-seat towns eager to industrialize. The entire section, about equidistant from the major cities of Nashville, Knoxville, and Chattanooga, lies within that elongated part of the country known as Appalachia.

From west to east, the physiography of the Upper Cumberlands progresses from small, round knolls to steep hills and ridges. Then comes a plateau as high as 3,500 feet, which abruptly ends in an escarpment plunging 800 to 1,400 feet. The last feature effectively divides the region from industrial East Tennessee.

Until very recently, commerce and industry found the geography of the Upper Cumberlands too difficult to deal with and bypassed the region, leaving it in semi-isolation. The upper reaches of the Cumberland River were too shallow for tugs and barges. The major highway into the region was a two-lane blacktop road that almost doubled back on itself as it snaked along the ridges from east to west. A short-line railroad, the Tennessee Central, served the Upper Cumberlands until 1968 when it was forced to declare bankruptcy and was absorbed by three connecting lines. North-south travel was entirely dependent on

1

secondary roads, even more crooked and discouraging than the east-west route.

Access to the region is easier today, thanks largely to an interstate highway that cuts through the heart of the Upper Cumberlands on its way from Nashville to Knoxville. North-south automobile travel still is difficult, although secondary roads have been straightened and widened in most counties.

The early economy of the region was built around two perishable natural resources, timber and coal. As Jack Weller describes in his study of the Appalachian people, *Yesterday's People*, the entire highland area experienced a boom or bust economy, depending on demand for timber and coal. Although there were some good times, relatively speaking, the region's natural resources were steadily depleted during the first half of the twentieth century. The last boom came during the Second World War; after that, the coal industry was forced to automate to meet the increasing competition from other forms of energy. The small mines of Appalachia, including those of the Upper Cumberlands, became unprofitable and were closed by operators without much thought for what would become of the miners. Many men who knew nothing but coal mining were thrown out of work. Some tried to find new lives in the industrial cities of the North, such as Chicago, Dayton, and Toledo. Many could not adjust and returned to their native hills. Others could not leave the protection of the only home they had ever known. Unable to find work, they gardened or stayed at home while wives worked in garment factories that sought cheap labor in the region. Some men become psychological cripples and a source of irritation and frustration to professional and business classes; even today, while many of the growing middle class of the Upper Cumberlands is conscientiously concerned with what to do about the poverty in its midst, others are convinced that the poor often would prefer drawing welfare than working for an honest living.

Isolation, poor transportation, and thinning natural resources affected the region's economy and in turn led to limited financial support of education and a good deal of inbreeding of teachers. A study of the Upper Cumberland's needs, done in 1965 by two Tennessee universities, concluded:

Over half of the families in the Upper Cumberland region live below the minimum subsistence level of $3,000 established by the federal government. The effective per capita income of the region is 65 percent of the per capita income of the state of Tennessee, and only 49 percent of the per capita income of the United States.

Inadequate housing, poor sanitary conditions, a lack of personal cleaniness and grooming, and limited medical, dental and hospital care are prevalent in this region. Physician-population and dentist-population ratios for the Upper Cumberland region are more than twice as large as the same ratios for the state of Tennessee.

A low-income family environment tends to retard the social and mental growth of young children. These children are usually unable to compete in public schools with children from their peer group who have the advantages afforded by middle-class families. Children with a limited education and few job skills repeat the cycle of poverty.

Public school systems in the Upper Cumberland region are not meeting the needs of youth, especially non-college bound youth. Student drop-out rates are high, particularly for boys . . .

The public school systems in this region are inadequate in many ways. They have limited curriculums, poor facilities and limited funds. One-fourth of the teachers do not hold a bachelor's degree. Most of the teachers are natives of this region and have had little opportunity to observe or work in an effective school system.

More than half of the teaching staff has been teaching for more than fifteen years.

The basic question of how education can be improved in such an area under such conditions may be answered in several ways. One of the obvious solutions would be to concentrate on improving the teacher. Such an opportunity was afforded by the passage of the Elementary and Secondary Education Act, which was part of a package of Great Society legislation enacted by Congress in the sixties. The act, known as ESEA, had several sections. The one relevant to our purposes was entitled Title 3, which, in turn, had several objectives, one of those being to assist schools in demonstrating promising new practices, to evaluate them, and when finding them good, to make them broadly known (Pace Report, April 1968). A project was designed with three major components with funds from Title 3 resources. The first of these components was an in-service program, an evaluation of which is the subject of this report. The other two sections dealt with cultural guidance counseling aspects within the school system and will not be discussed here.

In-service in the Upper Cumberlands for years had featured the lecture-panel discussion approach to new teaching methods and materials. Little attempt had been made to involve listeners, and sometimes speakers from the professional lecture circuit were imported to address large groups.

Many meetings would close with an "evaluation" period, and the remarks made at these were mostly complimentary. Privately, however, many teachers complained of boring and uninteresting meetings that contained little of direct value to them. Planners of Project Upper Cumberland envisioned a new kind of in-service training, utilizing the sensitivity training approaches. The project lasted over three years. It began in the summer of 1967, when 150 participants representing all sixteen counties in the region met for a period of two weeks and for fifteen meetings during the subsequent weeks of the year. The first year, no evaluation took place as the funding came too late for such planning to take place. In the summer of 1968, another 150 participants went through a two-week period of sensitivity training and also met for fifteen weekly meetings designed to help the participants learn to apply what they had learned in

4

the workshop to their "back home" situations. An evaluation of the effects of this sensitivity training was undertaken, and the project is described in the following pages. Developments at national and state levels led to the budget for the third year of the project being drastically cut so that the number of participants was reduced to seventy-five. The third workshop in the summer of 1969 was designed as a period of retraining for some of the more promising participants from the first two years of the program. All participants in the first two years were nominated by their respective school superintendents. The third-year selection was made by the workshop trainers and the leaders of the weekly meetings. It was hoped that these would work as co-trainers with leaders from regional universities and that the local systems could thus afford to incorporate some of the human relations training into their in-service programs. There were no follow-up meetings in the last year.

Participants in all three years of the program were paid stipends based on those established for institutes held under the National Defense Education Act. They received fifteen dollars for each day they attended, plus two dollars a day for each dependent other than themselves. The following pages will detail the evaluative aspects of the Cumberland project and report the results of the endeavor.

Chapter II

THE ASSESSMENT PROJECT

As mentioned earlier, the project planners decided that the teacher, being a very significant determinant of the quality of education, would be the target of their efforts. A number of investigators have felt that an educator's skills in the area of interpersonal relationships, his personality characteristics, and his value systems are more important than his professional training. Barr (1935), after a review of the research, concluded that the qualities that are readily measured, such as knowledge of subject matter and mastery of teaching skills, are overshadowed by the difficult-to-measure and more subtle variables of the teacher's personality, interpersonal relationships, and the whole area of student-teacher and teacher-teacher relationships. Combs (1965) later arrived at the same conclusion.

Other writers have emphasized and underlined the importance of interpersonal relationships. Anderson and Brewer (1945) talked about the "integrative" behavior of educators as being of central importance. In the fifties, several writers such as Bush (1954) and Moustakas (1956) gave support to the argument and emphasized the interpersonal skills of the teacher as an extremely important variable in his or her effectiveness. Prescott (1958) stated that the primary condition for an effective relationship with a student is the recognition by the teacher of feelings and attitudes peculiar to himself and the pupil and how these are influenced by special conditions of his life. Cogan (1958) demonstrated that authoritarianism was a crucial variable in educator functioning. Several attempts were made to demonstrate the importance of these variables in the student-teacher relationship as well as the teacher-teacher relationship. Some of the notable attempts were by Flanders (1965), Getzels and Jackson (1963), and Gump (1964). Gump's studies pointed out that the less controlling the teacher is the better the student performs.

In recent years, the popularity of the sensitivity training movement that grew out of National Training Laboratories experiences at Bethel, Maine, and at other parts of the country have led to the belief that "one of the most effective means yet discovered for facilitating constructive learning, growth, and change—in individuals or organizations they compose—is the intensive group experience" (Rogers, 1967). The literature on the sensitivity training group has been fairly extensive and reviewed at length by Bradford (1958) and Gibb and Durhan (1964). When the sixties saw the rising popularity of the sensitivity training movement, a few attempts were made to assess the effect of such training on teachers (Wedell, 1957; Mathis, 1955). Argyris (1962), using descriptive criteria, found that participants in sensitivity training were able to describe other members of the group in interpersonal terms after the group experience.

The most critical review of the effectiveness of sensitivity training was carried out by Odiorne (1963). His main contention was that there was little real definitive research other than by Bowers (1962) and Argyris (1962) to show that training is effective in changing people in the areas in which they function. Since Odiorne's review, additional research on the effects of training have been attempted (Stock in Bradford, 1964; Knowles, 1967). However, there does not seem to be any study that concerned itself with the assessment of the effects of sensitivity training on the functioning of educators who came from the kind of region described above. Moreover, these studies had not attempted to use a control group to see the differential effect among such groups.*

The present study was an attempt, therefore, to assess the value of the sensitivity training in as varied and extensive a fashion as possible. As every researcher knows, what is desirable and what is attainable because of practical limitations are not always the same. Such was the case in the present undertaking. In the first year of the program, a group of educators, recommended by their superiors for human relations training, were sent to a central location where they went through two weeks of such training and subsequently met for fifteen Saturdays. At this stage, no attempt was made to assess carefully the effect of this training except through the administration of a hurriedly prepared feedback questionnaire.

During the second year, 150 participants went through a similar experience. At this time, a comparatively comprehensive assessment program was instituted. Following Martin (1957) and Campbell and Dunnett (1968), a distinction between internal and external criteria for change was made, and the present program attempted to study the results of the sensitivity training along both these dimensions. Several attempts have been made to study these changes but without the use of control groups (Bennis et al., 1957; Burke and Bennis, 1961.) The present study, by use of a control group, attempted to study the differential effect of the training program brought about in the participants of the workshops.

Internal criteria were measured through various personality tests, which will be described at length in the following pages. The external criteria involved the effect of the training on those who came in contact with the participants. Testing involving the internal criteria was done at three points. The participants were tested just prior to their undergoing the human relations training (Pretest 1), just after the training (Post-

*Since this report was written, related research in this area has been described by Morton A. Liebierman, Irvin D. Yalom, and Matthew B. Miles in *Encounter Groups: First Facts* (New York: Basic Books, 1973).

test 1) and after a period of six months (Post-test 2). The control group of fifty went through similar procedures at Pretest and Post-test 1. Practical financial limitations led to an elimination of Post-test 2 for the control group.

During the third year of the program, only seventy-five participants were involved in a series of human relations training techniques. These participants gave subjective reactions to the program at the end of the three weeks.

The results of the project will be described in two broad sections. The first section will deal with the assessment program for the second year. It will describe the measures included under the internal and the external criteria. The second section will describe the measurements undertaken during the third year that were assumed to comprise both internal and external criteria.

We will not attempt to describe at length the nature of the sensitivity training. It may be stated that the exact techniques varied over the three-year-period as they did over the two-year-period with which the assessment was involved. The trainers themselves changed because of personal and administrative reasons that are beyond the scope of this report. The experience with the teachers after the first year led to some modification and expansion of the program in the second year and, subsequently, in the third year. The trainers themselves did not specify the goals of the training. The goals were, therefore, assumed to be those referred to in the literature of the sensitivity training. As is commonly recognized, the assumed changes wrought by the sensitivity training range from value systems to deeper and more permanent personality dimensions. In order to maximize the possibility of tapping any or all of these changes, the measures used were those derived from several personality theory models, such as those espoused by Lewin, Maslow, Cattel, and the general humanistic writers. Specifically, these were also chosen for their established reliability and validity and for practical reasons for ease of administration. All of the measures could be group administered, which was a major practical consideration. The measures were as follows: (1) Authoritarianism

Scale (F Scale) (Adorno, Brunswik-Frankel, Levinson, and Sanford, 1950), (2) Leary Interpersonal Check List (Leary, 1956), (3) the Personal Orientation Inventory (Shostrom, 1966), (4) Semantic Differential (Osgood, Suci, and Tannenbaum, 1955), (5) the Motivation Analysis Test (Cattel, Horn, Sweeny, and Radcliffe, 1964). Each of these instruments will be described in the following pages.

The external criteria comprise those changes that can be assumed to take place in the external environment of an individual. For example, the effect that a teacher may have on his/her students as a result of his/her exposure to the sensitivity training or the effect that an educator may have on the community around him/her are classified as external criteria changes. The project in question used three instruments in order to assess these changes: (1) ratings by principles (Ryan's Teacher Rating Scale, 1960), (2) selected cards from the Michigan Picture Test and the Thematic Apperception Test (Murray), (3) the Leary Interpersonal Check List to assess the students' perceptions of the teachers and of themselves. These measures will also be described in the following pages.

The assessment during the third year consisted of a feedback questionnaire and of open-ended clinical interviews that aimed at getting information regarding both types of changes, that is, those assumed to have taken place within the teachers themselves as well as in the communities in which they functioned. These will be presented in a separate section.

SECTION ONE

Chapter III

INTERNAL CRITERIA

This chapter will describe the various measures used to assess the internal criteria for the second-year group and present the results for each of the instruments. To recapitulate, these measurements were made prior to the sensitivity training (Pretest) for both the experimental and control groups immediately after the training for the experimental group (Post-Test 1) and six months later (Post-Test 2) for both groups. In effect, then, we have three measurements for the experimental group and two for the control group. The major comparisons were concerned with the difference in the changes between the two groups from the first testing (Pretest) to the last (Post-test 2). As we shall see later, some of the changes in the experimental group did not surface immediately after the sensitivity training experience (Post-test 1) but six months later at the time of Post-test 2.

F Scale

The first of the tests to be considered is Authoritarianism—the F Scale. The literature on this scale has been voluminous and will not be reviewed. However, it is interesting to recall the definition of high authoritarianism, given by the authors, which may well be assumed to be contrary to the goals of sensitivity training. High scores on the F Scale consist of the following (Adorno et al., 1950, pages 255—256):

A. *Conventionalism*: adherence to conventional middle class values.
B. *Authoritarian submission*: submissive, uncritical attitude towards idolized moral authorities of the in-group.
C. *Authoritarian aggression*: tendency to be on the lookout for and to condemn, reject and punish people who violate conventional values.
D. *Anti-introception*: opposition to subjective, imaginative and the tender minded.
E. *Superstition and stereotypes*: belief in the mystical determinants of individuals' fate, the disposition to think in rigid categories.
F. *Power and toughness*: preoccupation with dominance-submission, strong-weak, leader-follower dimensions; identification with power figures; over-emphasis upon the conventional as attributes of the ego; exaggerated exertion of strength and toughness.
G. *Destructiveness and cynicism*: generalized hostility, vilification of the human.
H. *Projectivity*: disposition to believe that wild and dangerous things go on in the world.
I. Sex: A concern with sexual goings-on.

As may be recalled, the F Scale was administered three times to the experimental group and twice to the control group. The initial scores for the two groups were not significantly different. The mean F Scale score for the control group was 116 and 112 for the experimental. A ratio between these two means was 1.084, which is not significant at the 5 percent level. The scores for both the groups changed somewhat, but the mean change score for the control group from the first to the second administration—that is, from Pretest to Post-test 2— was plus .167. A t test of significance for paired samples (Guilford, 1965) was computed; the value of t was 0.567, which is not significant. However, for the experimental group, the mean change in the F score from the first to the third administration was minus 5.22. The t ratio was minus 3.179, which is significant at .001 level. The results indicate that the experimental group changed significantly toward a lower score on the F Scale, whereas the control group did not change. In view of the definition of the meaning of high scores on the F Scale, it seems obvious that the teachers became less authoritarian and less rigid in their thinking. Interestingly, the F Scale scores for the experimental group from the first to the second testing, that is, immediately prior and subsequent to the sensitivity training, did not change. However, the change, as it were, went through an incubation period and surfaced six months later.

Demographic variables, particularly concerned with age, sex, marital status, educational level, income, etc., were also examined with regard to their relationship with the changes in the F Scale. Regression equations were computed between the two sets of data. The only significant relationships were those between income level and the number of years in the profession. It seems that the greater the number of years in the profession, the less a person changes as far as the dimensions of authoritarianism are concerned. In addition, it also seemed that the higher an individual's income, the more he changed in his attitudes. None of the other demographic variables seemed to play any significant role in the changes measured by this instrument.

Interpersonal Checklist (ICL)

Leary and his associates (1956) derived this checklist from his theoretical system of personality (1956). However, the ICL has been widely researched and used. It consists of 128 items representing eight interpersonal traits. The phrases may be used for description of self or others. Thus, it lends itself to comparisons of differing perceptions and has been used both for research and clinical purposes.

The eight interpersonal traits are described in Appendix

A. These can be scored at the octant level or at higher levels. In order to facilitate the behaviorial interpretation of the checklist, only the octant scores were used.

The changes in the self-perceptions were very striking in the experimental group and generally insignificant for the control group.

TABLE 1

Means and Standard Deviations,
Experimental Group, Interpersonal
Checklist (N-94)

Scale	Pretest	Post-Test 1	Post-Test 2
AP	Mean - 5.52 S.D. - 2.69	5.33 2.81	4.70 2.74
BG	Mean - 5.97 S.D. - 2.17	5.84 2.31	5.72 2.53
DE	Mean - 6.57 S.D. - 2.67	6.28 2.50	6.04 2.57
FG	Mean - 4.43 S.D. - 2.25	4.17 2.22	3.77 2.12
HI	Mean - 6.55 S.D. - 2.94	6.16 2.82	5.23 2.67
JK	Mean - 7.97 S.D. - 2.46	7.56 2.84	6.76 2.61
LM	Mean - 8.65 S.D. - 3.12	8.43 3.12	7.79 2.88
NO	Mean - 8.56 S.D. - 2.81	8.20 3.16	7.51 3.17

TABLE 2

Test of Significance of Changes in
Experimental Group Mean Scores (ICL)

Scale	Pretest vs. Post-test 1	Post-test 1 vs. Post-test 2	Pre- vs. Post-test 2
AP	NS	$p < .05$	$p < .01$
BC	NS	NS	NS
DE	NS	NS	$p < .05$
FG	NS	$p < .05$	$p < .05$
HI	NS	$p < .01$	$p < .05$
JK	NS $p < .10$	$p < .01$	$p < .01$
LM	NS	$p < .05$	$p < .05$
NO	NS	$p < .05$	$p < .05$

The experimental group changed their self perceptions significantly in seven of the octants (Tables 1 and 2). In view of the descriptions of the octants, one may conclude that the educators changed along the following dimensions.

1. They saw themselves as forceful leaders. They liked responsibility and giving orders. They stated that they were able to give orders and command respect of others.
2. They viewed themselves as being more straightforward and direct. They felt that they were more frank and honest and firm but just in their decisions.
3. They reported to have become less rebellious and less distrustful of others. They felt that they had the ability to complain in a realistic manner whenever necessary.
4. They said that they were less timid and less self-punishing. They said that they were able to look at themselves realistically and criticize themselves if necessary.

5. They reported that they had been able to develop a realistic respect for authority, and they became more appreciative of the help of others.
6. They viewed themselves as being more sociable and neighborly and made a conscious effort to get along with others. They also saw themselves as friendly and cooperative.
7. They viewed themselves as giving more freely of themselves and helpful to others. They also felt they became more considerate.

An additional finding concerning the changes in the experimental group was that the changes tended to occur at some time after training was over rather than immediately after the two-week training laboratory. No significant differences in scores occurred between the pretest and the first post-test. Yet when the pretest is compared with the second post-test, the differences noted above appeared. This is congruent with other theories of personal change as a result of group experience in that the application of new interpersonal skills acquired "in group" have a cumulative effect over time to change self-concept gradually as positive "back home" experiences are built up.

In contrast, the control group did not show any significant changes in the majority of the octants (Table 3). There were significant changes in one of the octants. The intervening period of six months appears to have made the control group feel that they are respectful of authority, grateful and appreciative.

Further Analysis of the F Scale and ICL

When the initial analysis of our data revealed a number of very significant changes in the mean scores of the experimental group on both the F Scale and the Leary Interpersonal Checklist, it was decided to continue the analysis by correlational methods in an attempt to discover what variables were related to these changes. An additional hope was to understand the effects of a group experience in a group of strangers (heterogeneous

TABLE 3

Control Group, Pre- and Post-Test 2
Results on Interpersonal Checklist
With Significance Tests

Scale	Pretest	Post-Test 2	Significance of Change
AP	Mean – 4.93	4.96	NS
	S.D. – 2.64	2.36	
BC	Mean – 5.60	5.60	NS
	S.D. – 2.24	1.91	
DE	Mean – 5.67	5.56	NS
	S.D. – 2.25	2.16	
FG	Mean – 3.18	3.40	NS
	S.D. – 2.28	2.04	
HI	Mean – 5.13	4.96	NS
	S.D. – 2.61	2.48	
JK	Mean – 6.51	5.49	$p < .01$
	S.D. – 2.17	1.85	
LM	Mean – 8.02	7.38	NS
	S.D. – 3.22	2.69	
NO	Mean – 7.67	7.44	NS
	S.D. – 2.89	2.89	

groups) versus a group made up of coworkers from "back home" (homogeneous groups). This analysis was done in two steps, with the first being a complete correlation study of all variables involved and the second being a multiple regression attempt at predicting the changes in both the F Scale and the Leary Checklist Scales.

The prediction variables were eleven demographic characteristics, including (Table 4) age, marital status, sex, number of professional years in education, number of years as a teacher, number of nonteaching (administrative) years, number of years in college, income in thousands, number of dependents, population of the town of residence, and whether or not the subject received supplemental salary from either moonlighting or extra

TABLE 4

Intercorrelations of Predictor Variables

Variables	2	3	4	5	6	7	8	9	10	11	12
1. Age in Years	-.00	0.09	.81	.76	.21	.01	-.04	-.14	-.24	-.14	.05
2. Marital Status (1= Married 0= Single)		.11	.06	.01	.10	-.08	-.06	.11	.08	-.03	-.20
3. Sex (1= Male 0= Female)			-.04	-.16	.33	.19	.37	.50	.07	.50	-.17
4. Number of professional Years				.90	.32	.16	-.01	-.20	-.10	-.14	.04
5. Number of Teaching Years					.03	.10	-.09	-.15	-.22	-.15	.12
6. Number of Non-Teaching Years						.20	.13	.07	.06	.16	-.09
7. Number of College Years							.31	.00	-.00	.14	-.04
8. Income (in 1,000's)								.14	.01	.29	-.11
9. Number of Dependents									-.20	.38	.08
10. Population of Town of Residence										.02	-.26
11. Supplemental Salary (1= Yes, 0= No)											.11
12. Group (1= Heterogeneous 0= Homogeneous)											

18

teaching duties such as coaching. An additional variable was the kind of group the subject was in. The other prediction variables used were the raw scores at the initial testing of each scale. This variable was included since it was felt that initial level on any given scale would be important in understanding the direction and magnitude of change in that scale.

As our criteria scores for prediction, three indices of change were computed for each scale, the first being an overall change score derived from the difference between the initial level on the scale and the second post-testing. This score will be referred to in this analysis of the test scores as the "overall change" score. The second criterion score is derived from the difference in scores between the pretest and the first post-testing, which followed immediately after the training sessions. This score will be referred to in the future as the "within session" change. The third score for each scale is derived from the change between the end of the training sessions (i.e., first post-test) and the second post-test, the time between the end of training and the follow-up six months later. This score will be designated "between" score in the body of the report. These criteria scores were derived by means of subtraction, so that a negative change score indicates a decrease in overall score, while a positive change score indicates an increase in score. For example, a subject who scored 110 on the F Scale pretest and who scored 105 on the first post-test immediately after training would have a within session change score of minus 5. This fact must be kept in mind in interpreting the sign of the correlation coefficients derived.

The correlation analysis contains forty-eight variables: eleven demographic characteristics, group membership, three scores each for the F Scale and the eight subscales of the Leary Checklist, and the nine pretest scores for the F Scale and the Leary Checklist. A correlational analysis of this forty-eight variable problem was carried out on an IBM-360 Model 40 Computer, utilizing a multiple regression and correlation program called the BMD-02R, developed and revised by the Health Sciences Computing Facility of UCLA. The resulting 48 × 48 correlation matrix and 27 prediction equations provided the hard data for this section of this report.

General Findings of the Correlation Matrix

To attempt to interpret a correlation matrix of this size containing some 1400 correlations is at best a complex and difficult proposition. To make this process more understandable, the matrix had to be broken down into manipulable parts. In addition, there is the problem in a matrix of this size of artifactual correlations of significant size occurring purely by chance. To minimize this latter problem, no correlation smaller than .20 (the .05 level of significance) was interpreted as a relationship, and those that were greater than this size were interpreted with great caution. The reader is reminded that a correlational relationship is in no way indicative of a causative relationship and must be interpreted with great caution in a single sample study. Another caution is that any prediction equation cannot be taken as fact until it has been cross-validated on an independently drawn sample from the same population.

With these cautions in mind, the overall matrix was subdivided into meaningful divisions for analysis. The first area of interest for any correlational study is the intercorrelation of one's predictor variables since independence of these variables is important for accurate prediction. As can be seen from Table 4, the correlations range from essentially zero to the artificially inflated value of .90. There are, however, some moderate relationships that do not appear to be artifactual that deserve comment. Besides the artifactual high correlation between age and number of professional years and number of teaching years, there appears to be a moderate relationship between sex and number of nonteaching (administrative) years, suggesting that more males go into the administrative field. Sex seems to be related in a positive way to being an administrator, having a higher income, having a larger number of dependents, and receiving supplemental salary. In any case, the independence of

20

the variables is somewhat limited, which probably lowers their ability to predict changes to a great extent.

TABLE 5

Correlations of Predictors and
Changes in F Scale

Variables	Overall Change In F Scale	Changes In Session	After Session
1. Age in Years	.04	.05	-.00
2. Marital Status (1= Married 0= Single)	-.09	.04	-.11
3. Sex (1= Male 0= Female)	-.21	-.01	-.18
4. Number of Professional Years	.09	.09	.01
5. Number of Teaching Years	.10	.03	.06
6. Number of Non-Teaching Years	-.05	.02	-.05
7. Number of College Years	-.04	-.07	.03
8. Income (in 1000's)	-.30	-.23	-.08
9. Number of Dependents	-.15	-.15	-.02
10. Population of Town of Residence	-.03	-.05	.02
11. Supplemental Salary (1= Yes 0= No)	-.28	-.04	-.22
12. Group (1= Heterogeneous 0= Homogeneous	.05	.08	-.03

The next attempt at analysis involved the correlations of the twelve demographic variables with changes in the various scales. Table 5 shows the correlations of these variables with changes in the F Scale. In overall changes, it will be noted that only sex, income, and supplemental salary are significantly related to change. Note also that the kind of group used is in no way related to changes in the F Scale. This suggests that authoritarianism was reduced independent of knowing or not knowing the members of one's sensitivity training group. All the relationships noted are negative, suggesting that of these predictors those most associated with decreases in score are being male, having a higher than average (for this sample) income and receiving supplemental salary. The other correlations on this table are small and probably not overly useful in prediction.

Table 6 shows the same information for the eight subscales of the ICL, covering only the overall changes. In interpreting these correlational values, it is a necessity to keep in mind what each scale attempts to measure. In Scale AP, which relates to managerial-autocratic kinds of self-perception, being male, having less than average education, and being in a stranger group were associated with decreases in score. In Scale BC, related to competitive kinds of self-perception, only being in a stranger group seemed to be related to decreases in score. No significant correlations appeared in Scales DE or FG. Scale HI, however, having to do with self-effacing, masochistic kinds of attitudes, seemed to have decreases in score related to being younger than average, having less experience, not being an administrator, and being in a heterogeneous group. JK, a scale having to do with submission and being dependent, showed decreases in the younger, less experienced numbers of the subject poll. For Scale LM, having to do with being cooperative and overly conventional, the only significant relationship was with number of nonteaching years, suggesting that the nonadministrators were more likely to decrease in score on this variable. Scale NO showed no significant correlations. The lack of large numbers of significant correlations in this table suggest that our

TABLE 6

Correlations of Predictors With Overall Changes in ICL

Variables	AP	BC	DE	FG	HI	JK	LM	NO
1. Age in Years	.14	.18	.10	.05	.22	.17	.11	.02
2. Marital Status (1= Married 0= Single)	-.00	.04	.07	.04	-.04	.01	-.08	-.19
3. Sex (1= Male 0= Female)	-.21	-.11	.01	-.05	-.19	-.18	-.02	-.15
4. Number of Professional Years	.05	.13	.13	.04	.30	.26	.19	.01
5. Number of Teaching Years	.07	.11	.10	.04	.25	.19	.16	.02
6. Number of Non-Teaching Years	.02	.10	.11	-.01	.25	.27	.24	-.02
7. Number of College Years	-.28	-.11	-.13	-.04	.08	.11	.06	.03
8. Income (in 1000's)	-.12	-.15	-.02	-.05	-.00	.05	.10	.06
9. Number of Dependents	-.04	-.06	.04	-.04	-.05	-.10	-.05	-.09
10. Population of Town of Residence	-.00	.03	.04	.00	-.21	-.06	-.06	-.13
11. Supplemental Salary (1= Yes, 0= No)	-.14	-.13	.12	-.17	.02	.04	.05	-.12
12. Group (1= Heterogeneous 0= Homogeneous)	.22	.21	.16	-.08	.20	.15	-.10	.02

efforts at predictions of changes from these demographic variables are slated for large disappointments without the inclusion of some other more highly correlated variables. However, the correlations that are significant in this table do appear to be meaningful relationships and make sense in terms of interpretation.

TABLE 7

Intercorrelations of Pretest Raw Scores
on the Leary Interpersonal Checklist
and Correlations With F Scale Pretest

	BC	DE	FG	HI	JK	LM	NO	F
AP	.62	.59	.35	-.02	.13	.21	.24	.09
BC		.57	.40	-.01	.12	.20	.15	.09
DE			.60	.14	.22	.12	.20	.03
FG				.35	.43	.21	.27	.14
HI					.63	.39	.30	.10
JK						.58	.53	.17
LM							.68	.33
NO								.28

In an effort to find other more reliable predictors, it was felt that the level of the initial score would be related to changes in that score over time. For this purpose, the pretest raw scores on each scale were included as a predictor of that scale. The intercorrelations of these scores for the ICL list and the correlations of the ICL with the F Pretest are shown in Table 7. The results are an interesting exercise in scale validation in that the Leary Interpersonal Checklist was developed empirically to show clusters of related self-perceptions that should be correlated with each other but not with the other scales. This is exactly what was discovered in the analysis of these results. The highest correlations of these scales tend to be those that are supposed to go together into the dominance and love composite scores. The dominance score comes from a composite of Scales AP, BC, DE, and FG. As may be noted, the intercorrelations of these four scales are higher than the correlations with the other four scales. On the other hand, the love score comes from a combination of HI, JK, LM, and NO. As may be noted again, the intercorrelations of these four scales are, in general, higher than the correlations with any of the other scales. This suggests that our subjects are, in fact, performing on this scale as they should.

An additional bit of information from Table 7 is that the F Scale is by and large uncorrelated with the interpersonal styles contained in the ICL. The only relationships that are significant are with Scales LM and NO. This is exactly what would be expected from the theoretical rationales of both the F Scale authoritarianism description and the two scales in question. Scale LM is supposedly related to overcooperative, overly conventional interpersonal attitudes, while NO has to do with being super-responsible and hypernormal. These should relate to the conventionality, stereotyped behavior, and rigidity of the authoritarian. The correlations are positive, as would be expected.

Table 8 shows the relationship between the demographic variables originally used as predictors and the pretest levels of both the F Scale and the Leary Interpersonal Checklist. First, high scores on the F Scale (indicating authoritarian attitudes) seem to be related to increased income, older than average age, higher than average professional years and teaching years, and inversely related to the amount of education. This suggests that, as might be expected from the kinds of attitudes that go into authoritarianism, the older one gets, the longer in one's profession, the less flexible and the more rigid one becomes. However, there is a tendency for education, with its exposure to more kinds of people and ideas, to moderate this effect and decrease the rigidity and conventionality associated with authoritarianism.

TABLE 8

Correlations of F Scale and Leary Interpersonal Checklist
Pretest Raw Scores With the Predictor Variables

Variables	F	AP	BC	DE	FG	HI	JK	LM	NO
1. Age in Years	.38	-.04	-.11	-.03	.09	.03	.09	.04	.18
2. Marital Status (1= Married 0= Single)	.05	-.01	-.08	-.15	.02	.06	.16	.24	.30
3. Sex (1= Male 0= Female)	-.08	.25	.19	.06	.16	-.07	-.12	-.11	-.09
4. Number of Professional Years	.34	-.00	-.10	-.02	.11	-.10	.02	-.03	.13
5. Number of Teaching Years	.34	-.07	-.16	-.01	.11	-.03	.03	.00	.12
6. Number of Non-Teaching Years	.13	.13	.16	.05	.06	-.20	-.01	-.13	.07
7. Number of College Years	-.21	.12	.14	.01	.01	-.19	-.09	-.03	.08
8. Income (in 1000's)	.01	.22	.28	.01	.05	-.13	-.12	-.08	-.07
9. Number of Dependents	-.04	.14	.12	.08	.25	-.03	.05	-.07	-.05
10. Population of Town of Residence	-.06	-.08	-.22	-.15	-.19	.12	.03	.02	-.00
11. Supplemental Salary (1= Yes, 0= No)	.04	.07	.15	.05	.12	-.16	-.05	-.05	.07
12. Group (1= Heterogeneous 0=Homogeneous)	-.02	.04	.10	.04	.11	-.02	.01	.16	.03

The correlations of the demographic variables with the ICL Scales are by and large not significant. There is a tendency for males to be more managerial and autocratic. In addition, those people with high incomes tend to be more managerial and autocratic and competitive. This is an expected and reasonable relationship. An additional interesting tendency, although not significant, is for sex (being male) to correlate positively with the scales associated with dominance and negatively with the scales associated with the love score. This relationship seems also expected in view of the cultural stereotypes of maleness and femaleness. The amazing thing is that the correlations are not larger since the part of the country from which the sample was drawn places great emphasis on the separateness and differentness of the male-female role model.

TABLE 9

Correlations of Pretest Raw Scores With Changes
(F Scale and Leary Checklist)

	Overall	Within	Between
F	-.51	-.32	-.19
AP	-.45	-.37	-.11
BC	-.43	-.38	-.13
DE	-.51	-.45	-.15
FG	-.55	-.39	-.28
HI	-.56	-.45	-.20
JK	-.35	-.25	-.08
LM	-.56	-.40	-.23
NO	-.36	-.30	-.08

Table 9 shows the correlations of the pretest scores with the changes in the scales in question. It will be noted that the correlations of the pretest scores with overall changes in score are all negative and quite substantial in size. Note also that the pretest level of scores also correlates significantly with changes within training session but not with changes between sessions after training. This difference has to do with the pattern of changes within the group, with many people increasing during the session and others decreasing but with an overall change

FIGURE 1

Direction of Changes in F Scale Scores
Within Session and During Follow-Up (Between) Period

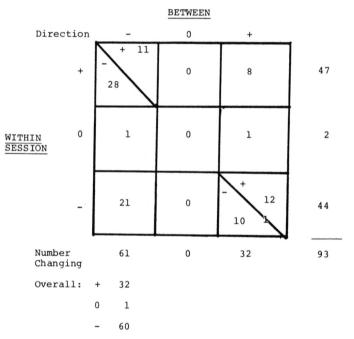

Note: The two diagonal cells (+ - and - +) show those individuals who showed both increases and decreases in score over the three testings. Those above the diagonal line had overall changes in scores that were positive and those below had overall changes in a negative direction. One subject (lower right cell) had equal increases and decreases to have an overall change of zero.

FIGURE 2

Results of Prediction of
Overall Changes in F Scale Scores

MULTIPLE R = .68   STANDARD ERROR OF ESTIMATE = 12.83

VARIABLES	COEFFICIENTS (BETA)
1. F Pretest	-.49
2. Income	-1.99
3. Number of Professional Years	.51
4. Sex	-5.04
5. Number of College Years	-3.36
6. Marital Status	-4.23

PREDICTED

DIRECTION	−	+	
+	13	19	32
REAL 0	1	0	1
−	54	6	60
			93

CORRECT PREDICTIONS: 54 of 60 who decreased

19 of 32 who increased

73 of 92 who changed

73 of 93 overall

toward decreased scores. This relationship is analyzed further
in Figures 1 and 2 of this report. In general, however, it may

be said that the relationship between the pretest score and the overall change is that those scoring high initially tend to decrease over time. Those scoring low tend to increase slightly, yielding a definite overall decrease in score.

At the other end of any prediction problem are the criteria measures, in this case the change scores for the various scales used. Table 10 shows the intercorrelations of the overall changes for the ICL. As was the case in the pretest scores, the correlations tend to fall in clusters with those scales most related to each other showing the highest correlation of change. This suggests that the more similar attitudes measured by two scales, the more alike their changes were.

TABLE 10

Intercorrelations of Overall Changes
in Leary's Self Concept Scale

	BC	DE	FG	HI	JK	LM	NO
AP	.55	.41	.30	.25	.27	.18	.17
BC		.50	.24	.30	.26	.23	.17
DE			.31	.31	.26	.16	.22
FG				.32	.26	.12	.09
HI					.62	.35	.17
JK						.43	.25
LM							.44
NO							

Table 11 shows the correlation of changes in a given scale within training, after training and overall. Again, the pattern of correlation is the same for all scales and may be generally characterized as a high positive correlation between the overall changes and changes after training, a relationship that could be expected from the changes in mean score. The unexpected result was the significant and quite large negative correlations between the changes within the session and those after the

30

session. This relationship suggests that in general people who increase in score during the session, decrease after they get out of the session and vice versa. This relationship was found to be true and is diagramed in Figures 3—10. This was the initial suggestion for the reasons for no significant change in mean score within the session. It suggested that there were subjects changing in a regular way but going in opposite directions during the two periods of measurement. That this was the case was an unexpected but helpful result in understanding the changes in means.

TABLE 11

Intercorrelations of Changes
(Overall, Within Session, and Post Session)

F Scale	In Session	Post Session
Overall	.32	.64
In Session		-.53

Interpersonal Checklist		
AP Overall	.39	.62
In Session		-.48
BC Overall	.36	.70
In Session		-.42
DE Overall	.47	.66
In Session		-.35
FG Overall	.54	.66
In Session		-.27
HI Overall	.53	.61
In Session		-.35
JK Overall	.34	.56
In Session		-.59
LM Overall	.52	.59
In Session		-.38
NO Overall	.41	.59
In Session		-.49

31

The most ready generalization from the findings is that the demographic characteristics chosen are not particularly good predictors of changes in the two scales used. It does, however, show that the attitudes measured in the Interpersonal Checklist and the F Scale are relatively independent of each other and a finding not yet reported in the literature.

The next section of this report is devoted to a very important problem in training groups—that is, how to predict how many and which individuals are going to benefit from training.

Interpretation of the Multiple Regression Analysis

Because of the independence of the two scales, it was decided to analyze the prediction equations and prediction results for the F Scale separate from the ICL. Because of the complex changes hinted at by the intercorrelations of the changes in the F Scale, the direction of the changes both within the session and between the session were cross-plotted on the chart shown in Figure 1. This chart shows that within the session forty-seven people increased in score, two remained the same, and forty-four decreased in score. This readily explains the non-significant change in mean score. However, during the follow-up period, noted here as between, sixty-one people decreased in score while thirty-two people increased. This is the reason for the negative correlation that occurred during this follow-up period. It is interesting to note, however, that there are sixty-one people of the ninety-three who showed both increases and decreases over the whole time period studied. These are shown in the diagonally marked corner cells of Figure 1.

Further analysis is needed to understand exactly the reasons for these changes and to discover what kinds of people consistently decrease, what kinds consistently increase, and those who show bidirectional changes. In any case, within this complex relationship of changes, it was felt that the change of interest to this experiment was the overall change in authoritarianism as a result of sensitivity training group experience.

Therefore, the analysis of the differential changes within session and following sessions were left for future analysis, and the prediction attempt was focused on the overall change in score.

Figure 2 shows the results of this multiple regression attempt. As may be seen from the figure, the resulting multiple correlation was .68, a fairly respectable figure. The standard error of estimate was 12.83, showing that our errors of prediction were fairly substantial. The variables used were the pretest score, income, number of professional years, sex, number of college years, and marital status. From the direction (sign of the beta coefficient), it may be seen that the variables connected with decreased scores on the F Scale are having a high pretest score, having higher than average income, being low in professional years, being male, having more education than usual, and being married. The variables are listed in order of relationship, and the latter two or three reflect very mild relationships. This result gives rise to several hypotheses, but the one that appears most likely is that those people who are more openly authoritarian at the outset of the training tend to become less so as a result of their new experiences and exposure to differing ideas and attitudes. On the other hand, those people who are defensive about their authoritarian attitudes initially become more open about their attitudes and thus increase slightly in score during the session. After the session, however, two-thirds of the subjects decrease in score, perhaps reflecting the application of new sensitivity and flexible attitudes learned in the group. This, of course, relates to the final result of decreased authoritarianism over the whole group. One of the problems with this hypothesis is that thirty-two people actually increased in authoritarianism over the whole time. Some of these decreased initially but went back up to their previous level or higher over the whole session. Others, eleven of them, increased initially but came back down to a score above their initial level. Only nine people actually continued to increase in authoritarianism over the whole time of the study. A scatter plot of the changes reveals, however, that these people were, by and large, people who scored lower than average on authoritarianism in the beginning and thus tends not to negate the hypothesis of less defensiveness and new experiences causing people to be more open about their attitudes and more flexible in their approach to other people.

The variables involved here suggest again what one would expect in dealing with authoritarian attitudes: that the older, the more conservative and the more experience a person has with a given social system, the more likely one is to absorb the socially accepted and conventional attitudes and the more rigid these attitudes become. The implications for sensitivity training are that these people who are more rigid benefit the most from the group experience in terms of decreased authoritarianism.

The results of prediction show that it is much easier to predict those people who decrease in score than it is to predict those who will increase. However, the overall prediction level is quite acceptable for the individual case. In this sample, the equation listed above correctly predicted seventy-three of the ninety-two subjects who changed in score over the whole time covered. This is a 79 percent accuracy and is probably acceptable as an increase rate in selecting subjects who will decrease in score, correctly picking fifty-four of the sixty.

Results of Prediction on the ICL

To begin the analysis of prediction on the ICL, the changes present were analyzed as to when and where they occurred, as was noted above in the F Scale. In the eight subscales of the ICL, the changes followed a pattern similar to that of the F Scale, as can be seen in Figures 3 through 10. In all scales, there were subjects going in both directions, both increasing and decreasing within their group sessions. These changes were approximately equal to being slightly more heavily weighted on the decrease side. This clearly explains the reason for the nonsignificant decreases in mean score during the group sessions. As in the F Scale, the changes during the follow-up or between period showed the same reversal of direction in as many as fifty of the cases out of ninety-three, but with a preponderance of decreasing scores. This leads to the overall result noted underneath the 3 × 3 charts (Figures 3–10) with forty-five to sixty-four of the ninety-three subjects showing an overall decrease in scores on the various scales.

FIGURE 3

Direction of Changes in Scale AP Within
Session and During Follow Up (Between) Period

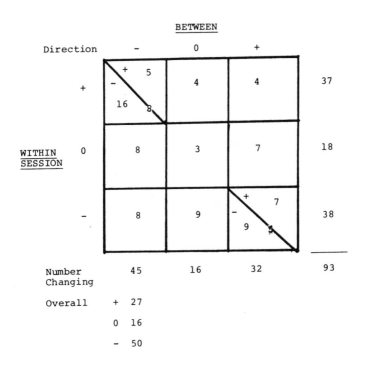

FIGURE 4

Direction of Changes in Scale BC Within
Session and During Follow Up (Between) Period

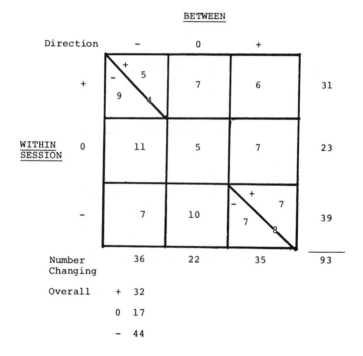

BETWEEN

Direction	−	0	+	
+	+ 5 / − 9 / 4	7	6	31
WITHIN SESSION 0	11	5	7	23
−	7	10	+ 7 / − 7 / 8	39
Number Changing	36	22	35	93

Overall   + 32

0 17

− 44

36

FIGURE 5

Direction of Changes in Scale DE Within
Session and During Follow Up (Between) Period

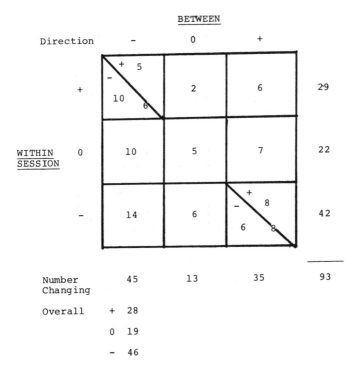

BETWEEN

Direction	−	0	+	
+	+ 5 / − 10 / 6	2	6	29
WITHIN SESSION 0	10	5	7	22
−	14	6	+ 8 / − 6 / 8	42
Number Changing	45	13	35	93

Overall + 28
         0 19
         − 46

37

FIGURE 6

Direction of Changes in Scale FG Within
Session and During Follow Up (Between) Period

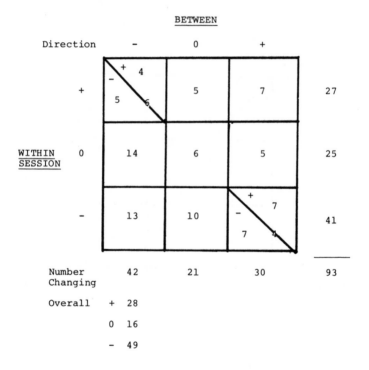

BETWEEN

Direction		-	0	+	
	+	+ 4 / - 5	5	7	27
WITHIN SESSION	0	14	6	5	25
	-	13	10	+ 7 / - 7	41
Number Changing		42	21	30	93
Overall	+	28			
	0	16			
	-	49			

38

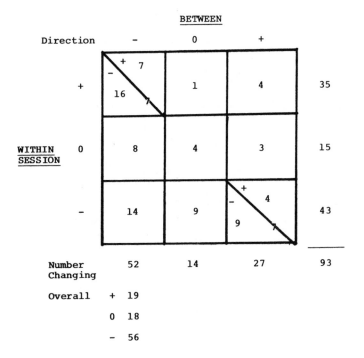

FIGURE 7

Direction of Changes in Scale HI Within
Session and During Follow Up (Between) Period

BETWEEN

Direction		−	0	+	
+		+ 7 / − 16	1	4	35
WITHIN SESSION	0	8	4	3	15
−		14	9	+ 4 / − 9	43
Number Changing		52	14	27	93

Overall   + 19

0 18

− 56

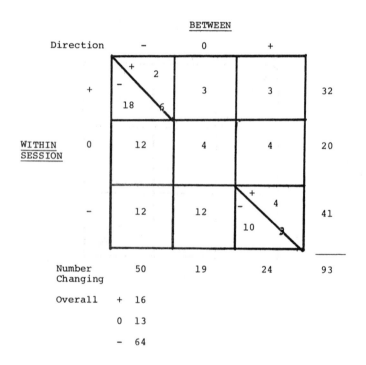

FIGURE 8

Direction of Changes in Scale JK Within
Session and During Follow Up (Between) Period

BETWEEN

Direction	−	0	+	
+	+ 2 / − 18 / 6	3	3	32
WITHIN SESSION 0	12	4	4	20
−	12	12	+ 4 / − 10 / 3	41
Number Changing	50	19	24	93

Overall + 16

0 13

− 64

FIGURE 9

Direction of Changes in Scale LM Within
Session and During Follow Up (Between) Period

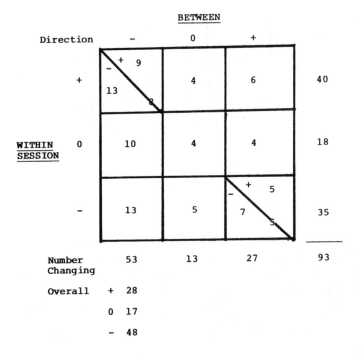

BETWEEN

Direction	–	0	+	
+	+ 9 / – 13 / 8	4	6	40
WITHIN SESSION 0	10	4	4	18
–	13	5	+ 5 / – 7 / 5	35
Number Changing	53	13	27	93

Overall	+	28
	0	17
	–	48

FIGURE 10

Direction of Changes in Scale NO Within
Session and During Follow Up (Between) Period

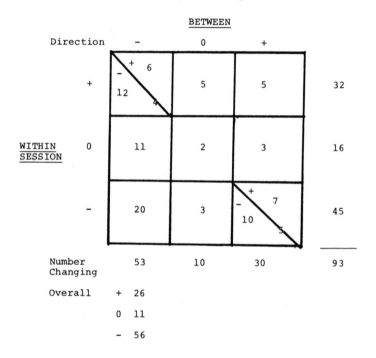

BETWEEN

Direction		−	0	+	
WITHIN SESSION	+	+ 6 − 12 4	5	5	32
	0	11	2	3	16
	−	20	3	+ 7 − 10 5	45
Number Changing		53	10	30	93

Overall	+	26
	0	11
	−	56

It is interesting to note that in Scale BC, the only scale that did not show significant change in mean score over the whole time, the number of subjects increasing and decreasing were relatively stable, so that people returned almost exactly to their pretest level over the whole time period. This result suggests that only about 50–60 percent of the subjects are showing decreases in their scores on the ICL. This suggests that perhaps this is the percentage of people who benefit from the limited group experience offered. This points out the drastic need for efficient prediction as to which people will show the decreases in score. This is the goal of the prediction equations listed in Figures 11–18. A suggestion for the interpretation of the

FIGURE 11

Results of Prediction of Overall
Changes in Scale AP

MULTIPLE R = .57   STANDARD ERROR OF ESTIMATE = 2.15

VARIABLES   COEFFICIENTS (BETA)

1. AP Pretest   -.43

2. Group   1.20

3. Number of College Years   -.84

4. Number of Nonteaching Years   .06

CONSTANT = 4.02

PREDICTED

Direction	−	+	
+	12	15	27
REAL 0	9	7	16
−	41	9	50
			93

CORRECT PREDICTIONS: 41 of 50 who decreased

15 of 27 who increased

56 of 77 who changed

56 of 93 overall

43

FIGURE 12

Results of Prediction of Overall
Changes in Scale BC

MULTIPLE R = .53   STANDARD ERROR OF ESTIMATE = 2.19

VARIABLES   COEFFICIENTS (BETA)

1. BC Pretest   -.57

2. Group   1.36

3. Number of Non Teaching Years   .08

CONSTANT = 2.21

PREDICTED

Direction	−	+	
+	13	19	32
REAL 0	6	11	17
−	34	10	44
			93

CORRECT PREDICTIONS: 34 of 44 who decreased

                       19 of 32 who decreased

                       53 of 76 who changed

                       53 of 93 overall

44

FIGURE 13

Results of Prediction of Overall
Changes in Scale DE

MULTIPLE R = .61   STANDARD ERROR OF ESTIMATE = 2.00

VARIABLES   COEFFICIENTS (BETA)

1. DE Pretest   -.48

2. Group   .96

3. Supplemental Salary   1.10

4. Number of Professional Years   .03

5. Number of College Years   -.62

6. Number of Nonteaching Years   .05

   CONSTANT = 3.62

PREDICTED

Direction	−	+	
+	11	17	28
REAL 0	9	10	19
−	39	7	46
			93

CORRECT PREDICTIONS: 39 of 46 who decreased

                       17 of 28 who increased

                       56 of 74 who changed

                       56 of 93 overall

45

FIGURE 14

Results of Prediction of Overall
Changes in Scale FG

MULTIPLE R = .59   STANDARD ERROR OF ESTIMATE = 1.82

VARIABLES   COEFFICIENTS (BETA)

1. FG Pretest   -.58

2. Supplemental Salary   -.81

3. Number of Dependents   .29

4. Number of Professional Years -   .02

   CONSTANT = 1.23

PREDICTED

Direction		−	+	
	+	10	18	28
REAL	0	10	6	16
	−	41	8	49

93

CORRECT PREDICTIONS: 41 of 49 who decreased

                       18 of 28 who increased

                       59 of 77 who changed

                       59 of 93 overall

46

FIGURE 15

Results of Prediction of Overall
Changes in Scale HI

MULTIPLE R = .70   STANDARD ERROR OF ESTIMATE = 2.03

VARIABLES   COEFFICIENTS (BETA)

1. HI Pretest   -.45
2. Number of Professional Years   .04
3. Sex   -1.81
4. Number of Nonteaching Years   .09
5. Group   .72
6. Population   -.06
7. Supplemental Salary   ..66

CONSTANT = .90

Direction	PREDICTED −	PREDICTED +	
+	7	12	19
REAL 0	10	8	18
−	52	4	56
			93

CORRECT PREDICTIONS: 52 of 56 who decreased

                      12 of 19 who increased

                      64 of 75 who changed

                      64 of 93 overall

47

FIGURE 16

Results of Prediction of Overall
Changes in Scale JK

MULTIPLE R = .63   STANDARD ERROR OF ESTIMATE = 1.69

VARIABLES   COEFFICIENTS (BETA)

1. JK Pretest   -.34

2. Number of Professional Years   .03

3. Sex   -2.05

4. Number of Nonteaching Years   .11

5. Supplemental Salary   1.02

6. Group   .63

7. Marital Status   .68

8. Income   .12

CONSTANT = -.51   PREDICTED

Direction   -   +

	+	11	5	16
REAL	0	11	2	13
	-	58	6	64

93

CORRECT PREDICTIONS: 58 of 64 who decreased

                        5 of 16 who increased

                       63 of 80 who changed

                       63 of 93 overall

48

FIGURE 17

Results of Prediction of Overall
Changes in Scale LM

MULTIPLE R = .62   STANDARD ERROR OF ESTIMATE = 2.38

VARIABLES   COEFFICIENTS (BETA)

1. LM Pretest   -.52

2. Number of Professional Years   .03

3. Number of Nonteaching Years   .08

4. Sex   -1.19

5. Supplemental Salary   .75

CONSTANT = 2.95

PREDICTED

Direction	−	+	
+	10	18	28
REAL 0	10	7	17
−	42	6	48
			93

CORRECT PREDICTIONS: 42 of 48 who decreased

18 of 28 who increased

60 of 76 who changed

60 of 93 overall

49

FIGURE 18

Results of Prediction of Overall
Changes in Scale NO

MULTIPLE R = .43   STANDARD ERROR OF ESTIMATE = 2.55

VARIABLES   COEFFICIENTS (BETA)

1. No Pretest   -.37

2. Sex   -1.30

3. Population   -.07

4. Income   .18

CONSTANT = 1.78

PREDICTED

Direction		-	+	
	+	18	8	26
REAL	0	7	4	11
	-	52	4	56
				93

CORRECT PREDICTIONS: 52 of 56 who decreased

8 of 26 who increased

60 of 82 who changed

60 of 93 overall

50

changes within session and between session is that the group session offered an intensive exposure to points of view quite different from the individual's normal social contacts. This led to a great upheaval or cognitive dissonance and some initial alterations, be they increased defensiveness and increased scores or temporary decreases induced by the intense interaction of the group setting. However, in the period following the sessions, the person is returned to his normal environment, and his old attitudes tend to reassert themselves, bringing him back toward his usual level of interaction or his usual style of relating to others. However, since the group sessions hopefully taught new ways of relating and new perceptions of self, the overall pattern for the group was a decrease in score.

Figures 11–18 show the multiple correlations derived, the standard error of estimate, the variables included in the prediction equation and their beta coefficients, and, finally, the outcome of the prediction equation in terms of correct prediction of direction of change. While this is a rather crude way of displaying the results, it gives a clear picture of how accurately the equations predict changes in this sample of subjects. Again the reader must be cautioned that these are tentative prediction equations and should not be used for actual application until they have been cross-validated.

As can be seen from Figures 11–18, the pretest scores are the strongest predictors of change. They appear in all of the prediction equations and are the heaviest contributors to the multiple correlation. Looking at the results of the prediction, it can be seen that the number of individuals correctly predicted ranged from fifty-three out of ninety-three to sixty-four out of ninety-three. It can also be noted that the lowest number predicted, fifty-three, was in Scale BC, in which there was no significant change in mean score. The multiple correlations ranged from about .5 through .7, all of which are significant regressions and useful in prediction where large groups of subjects are available. It further can be noted, from the overall accuracy tables, that it is much easier to predict the cases that will decrease than it is to predict those that will increase over the overall time period. The reasons for this differential pre-

51

diction are not readily apparent from the data presently available and should give rise to an inclusion of more variables in future research.

TABLE 12

Frequency of Occurrence of Predictor Variables
in Multiple Regression Equations for the
Leary Interpersonal Checklist
and Direction of Weight

Variables	Overall	Within Session	Post Session
1. Age			+++++
2. Marital Status	+	++	-
3. Sex	----	----	+-
4. Professional Years	+++++		+++-
5. Non Teaching Years (Administration)	++++++	+++	++
6. College Years	--	+++-	----
7. Income	++	----	+++
8. Number of Dependents	+		
9. Population of Town	--	-	-
10. Supplemental Salary	+-+++	++++++	---
11. Group	+++++	-	+++++
12. Pretest Raw Score	--------	--------	--------

In terms of specifying which variables are most useful in these predictions at present, Table 12 shows the frequency of appearance in the prediction equations of all the predictor variables used with the Leary Interpersonal Checklist. It also shows the direction of relationship in each appearance. It can be noted from this that all variables are not equally used. The pretest scores appear in the prediction of all eight scales for overall and within session and in all but one of the eight for the between, always in a negative relationship, suggesting that those people who score highest on the pretest are more likely to decrease in score. Other variables, like marital status, teaching years, number of dependents, and population, appear in very few prediction equations and appear to be not very useful in prediction of changes in the ICL. Of the demographic variables, number of professional years, longer experience in an administrative position, and receiving supplemental salary are less likely to decrease in score. In predicting the changes within session, the best predictors appear to be receiving supplemental salary, income, and sex, suggesting that males with good incomes and not receiving supplemantal salary are more likely to decrease within session.

In terms of changes during the follow-up or postsession period, the best predictors for change in this situation are age, college years, and group membership, with younger persons with higher education and receiving training in a stranger group showing the most likely decrease in scores.

In general, the results of the prediction and correlational study has offered some hope toward predicting the kinds of people who will benefit most from a sensitivity training experience. Although these results must be taken as tentative and subject to cross-validation on later independently selected samples, it is felt that the results point to the possibility of such selection being valuable. In general, it appears that there are two basic clusters or factors pointing toward decreases in score on the two instruments used here. The first of these is, of course, a pretest level that is in the upper extremes of the sample. In terms of authoritarianism, this means someone who is relatively authoritarian to begin with, before training. In terms of the ICL, it means someone who falls in the less desirable upper ends of the scale. The other factor tends to be one of flexibility, with those people who have more education and who are younger tending to benefit more.

Personal Orientation Inventory (POI)

One of the most influential humanist theorists, Abraham Maslow, with his idea of a self-actualizing person (Maslow, 1962), has been a major influence on the goals espoused by the

TABLE 13

Means and Standard Deviations of the Experimental
and Control Group on the Basis of Pretest

POI Item		PRETEST Experimental	Control	p
1. TI Time Incompetence	M	7.03	7.06	N.S.
	S	2.96	2.57	
2. TC Time Competence	M	15.84	15.76	N.S.
	S	2.95	2.66	
3. O Other Reactivity	M	47.89	48.02	N.S.
	S	9.63	8.92	
4. I Inner Reactivity	M	76.68	77.48	N.S.
	S	10.23	8.67	
5. SAV Self-Actualizing Value	M	19.34	19.54	N.S.
	S	2.59	2.35	
6. EX Existentiality	M	17.23	16.74	N.S.
	S	3.97	3.76	
7. FR Feeling Reactivity	M	13.80	13.32	N.S.
	S	2.71	2.70	
8. S Spontaniety	M	10.62	10.80	N.S.
	S	2.79	2.29	
9. SR Self Regard	M	11.68	12.06	N.S.
	S	2.30	2.60	
10. SA Self Acceptance	M	15.00	14.82	N.S.
	S	2.93	2.61	
11. NC Nature of Man	M	11.62	11.80	N.S.
	S	1.87	2.09	
12. SY Synergy	M	6.70	6.96	N.S.
	S	1.31	1.23	
13. A Acceptance of Aggression	M	14.70	14.52	N.S.
	S	3.28	3.24	
14. C Capacity for Intimate Contact	M	16.06	16.46	N.S.
	S	3.10	2.71	

M represents the Mean; S represents the Standard Deviation.
N for Experimental Group = 108; N for Control Group = 50.

Significance was computed on the basis of t-tests. Not significant implies a t-value which was not significant at 5% level.

sensitivity training movement. Maslow has pointed out "—there is today a standardized test of self actualization (The Personal Orientation Inventory). Self actualization can now be defined quite operationally, as intelligence used to be defined, that is, self actualization is what the test (POI) tests." (Maslow, 1967) Shostrom's Personal Orientation Inventory (1966) was, therefore, one of the other tests chosen for purposes of assessment in the project.

The POI has a number of subscales. These scales are briefly described in Appendix B. In line with Maslow's definition of self-actualization, these scales measure such dimensions as time competence, that is, the degree to which one is presently oriented, self-actualization value, existentiality, feeling reactivity, spontaneity, self-regard, self-acceptance, nature of man, synergy, acceptance of aggression, and capacity for intimate contact. In order to see if the two groups differed in any significant way prior to the sensitivity training, the means and standard deviations for the POI on the pretest for both the groups were examined, and no significant differences were found (Table 13).

Since the experimental group had been tested three times and the control group only twice, it was decided to deal with the differences in the groups separately. POI scores for the Pretest and the Post-test 2 of the control group were analyzed with the help of t ratios. No significance differences were found between the two testings (Table 14) so that we may conclude that the control group did not change along the dimensions measured by the POI.

The experimental group, on the other hand, did change in various ways. Newman-Keuls Test (Snedcore, 1956) of differences among means was used for the Pretest, Post-test 1 and Post-test 2. As Table 15 indicates, the participants changed significantly in all but three dimensions of the POI. They did not change their views with regard to an affirmation of the primary value of self-actualizing people (self-actualization value) or the "nature of man" dimension, which measures "degree of constructive view of the measure of man, masculinity femininity," and, finally, the dimension of synergy, which

TABLE 14

Means and Standard Deviations for the POI Scores
for the Pretest and the 2nd Post-Test of
the Control Group

		PRETEST			POST-TEST 2		
	POI	ITEM		POI	ITEM		p
1.	TI	M	77.06	TI	M	6.57	N.S.
		S	2.57		S	2.84	
2.	TC	M	15.76	TC	M	16.26	N.S.
		S	2.66		S	2.80	
3.	O	M	48.02	O	M	46.62	N.S.
		S	8.92		S	10.21	
4.	I	M	77.48	I	M	78.68	N.S.
		S	8.67		S	9.69	
5.	SAV	M	19.54	SAV	M	19.14	N.S.
		S	2.35		S	2.65	
6.	EX	M	16.74	EX	M	16.96	N.S.
		S	3.76		S	4.06	
7.	FR	M	13.32	FR	M	13.48	N.S.
		S	2.70		S	2.83	
8.	S	M	10.80	S	M	10.16	N.S.
		S	2.29		S	2.34	
9.	SR	M	12.06	SR	M	12.08	N.S.
		S	2.60		S	2.40	
10.	SA	M	14.82	SA	M	15.72	N.S.
		S			S		
11.	NC	M	11.80	NC	M	11.32	N.S.
		S	2.09		S	2.08	
12.	SY	M	6.96	SY	M	6.88	N.S.
		S	1.23		S	1.26	
13.	A	M	14.52	A	M	15.34	N.S.
		S	3.24		S	2.95	
14.	C	M	16.46	C	M	16.90	N.S.
		S	2.71		S	3.22	

M represents the Mean

S represents the Standard Deviation

measures the ability to transcend dichotomies. However, it
seems apparent that they did change in very significant ways
as a result of their experience. They became more time competent, which would imply that they were able to tie the past
and the future to the present in a more meaningful continuity.
It would also imply that they developed greater faith in the
future without rigid or overly idealistic goals. They were also

TABLE 15

Changes in the Experimental Group for the
Pretest, Post-Test 1 and Post-Test 2 on
the Basis of the Newman-Keuls Test
of Differences Among Means

	Item	p (using F distribution)	Means for the three testings*		
1.	TI	.01 .05	1 1	2 <u>2</u>	3 <u>3</u>
2.	Tc	.01 .05	1 <u>1</u>	2 <u>2</u>	3 3
3.	O	.01	1	<u>2</u>	<u>3</u>
4.	I	.01	1	<u>2</u>	<u>3</u>
5.	Sav	N.S.			
6.	Ex	.01	1	<u>2</u>	<u>3</u>
7.	Fr	.01	1	<u>2</u>	<u>3</u>
8.	S	.01	1	<u>2</u>	<u>3</u>
9.	Sr	.05	<u>1</u>	<u>2</u>	3
10.	Sa	.01	1	<u>2</u>	<u>3</u>
11.	Nc	N.S.			
12.	Sy	N.S.			
13.	A	.01	1	<u>2</u>	<u>3</u>
14.	C	.01	1	<u>2</u>	<u>3</u>

*1 = Pretest
 2 = Post-test 1
 3 = Post-test 2

Note: A line joining two numbers implies that the means were
not different.

more able to situationally or existentially react without rigid
adherence to principles (existentiality). They were able to react
with greater feeling, which would indicate sensitivity to one's
own needs and feelings. The self-regard of the experimental

group was enhanced in a marked fashion. The data also suggest that the self-acceptance was enhanced for the group. This would imply that they were able to accept themselves in spite of weaknesses or deficiencies and look at themselves more realistically. They became more aware, that is, they were better able to relate to all objects of life meaningfully. There was also an appreciable increase in the capacity for intimate contact with other human beings. They were better able to establish a more meaningful relationship with other human beings than they had been prior to this experience. Table 15 shows that most of the changes occurred immediately after the sensitivity training, that is, between the pretest and post-test. Only in two instances, namely, time competence and self-regard, did the change occur between the Post-test 1 and Post-test 2, again suggesting the kind of incubation period that was mentioned with regard to the F Scale.

The effect of the demographical variables, such things as years in profession, sex, age, and church affiliation, were ana-

TABLE 16

The Effect of Years in Profession on the
0 Subscale of the POI

Years	Pretest	Post-Test	N	Mean	Difference (Pre-Post)
0 - 9	43.46	37.15	26	40.30	6.31*
10 - 19	48.65	44.34	26	46.49	4.31*
20 - 29	50.55	44.52	40	47.53	6.03*
30 - Up	47.18	42.43	16	44.81	4.75*
	0 - 9, 30 - Up, 10 - 19, 20 - 29				

Note: A line joining two numbers implies that the means were not different.

* Difference is significant at 5% level.

lyzed by the use of Newman-Keuls test. This resulted in eighty-two analyses. Out of these, about twelve were found to be significant.

Table 16 gives the effects of years of profession on the changes brought about by the sensitivity training on the 0 subscale of the POI. It appears that persons who had spent between ten and twenty-nine years in the profession became more oriented to others as compared to persons who had spent less than nine years in the profession and those who had spent more than thirty years in the profession; that is, the extremes on the distribution did not change as much as the middle. A number of the significant findings in this connection were on the existential dimension of the POI. The particular implications of each of these relationships may be a fruitful source of speculation, but in view of the fact that these are embedded in a large number of analyses, no far-ranging inferences were made.

TABLE 17

The Effects of Age on the Ex Subscale of the POI

Age	Pretest	Post Test	N	Mean	Difference (Pre-Post)
20 - 29	19.71	22.71	14	21.25	3.00*
30 - 39	16.07	19.00	13	17.53	2.93*
40 - 49	16.90	20.30	33	18.60	3.40*
50 - Up	17.04	19.02	48	18.03	1.98*
	30 - 39, 50 - Up. 40 - 49, 20 - 29				

Note: A line joining two numbers implies that the means were not different.

* Difference is significant at 5% level.

Table 17 shows that persons between twenty and twenty-nine years of age became more existentially oriented. This age

59

group seemed to differ from all the other age groups. On this subscale, there seemed to be no difference in the amount of change, though it seems that males became slightly more existentially oriented than females (Table 18).

TABLE 18

The Effect of Sex on the Ex Subscale of the POI

Sex	Pretest	Post Test	N	Mean	Difference (Pre-Post)
Male	18.31	21.17	35	19.74	2.86**
Female	16.71	19.27	73	17.99	2.56**

** Difference is significant at 1% level.

TABLE 19

The Effect of Church Affiliation on the
Ex Subscale of the POI

Church Affiliation	Pretest	Post Test	N	Mean	Difference (Pre-Post)
Baptist	17.75	21.37	32	19.56	3.62**
Methodist	18.27	20.78	33	19.53	2.41**
Church of Christ	15.30	18.15	26	16.73	2/85**

Church of Christ, <u>Methodist, Baptist</u>

Note: A line joining two words implies that the means were not different

** Difference is significant at 1% level.

60

Table 19 indicates that Baptists or Methodists changed more than persons who belonged to the Church of Christ. Church affiliation was responsible for some differences in changes along the spontaneity dimension of the POI (Table 20).

TABLE 20

The Effect of Church Affiliation on the
S Subscale of the POI

Church Affiliation	Pretest	Post Test	N	Mean	Difference (Pre-Post)
Baptist	10.75	11.87	32	11.31	1.12*
Methodist	11.69	12.00	33	11.84	.31*
Church of Christ	9.65	10.96	26	10.30	1.31*

Church of Christ, Baptist, Methodist

Note: A line joining two words implies that the means were not different.

* Difference is significant at 5% level.

TABLE 21

The Effect of Church Affiliation on the
A Subscale of the POI

Church Affiliation	Pretest	Post Test	N	Mean	Difference (Pre-Post)
Baptist	15.62	16.81	32	16.21	1.19*
Methodist	15.45	16.33	33	15.89	.88*
Church of Christ	13.42	15.15	26	14.28	1.73*

Church of Christ, Methodist, Baptist

Note: A line joining two words implies that the means were not different.

* Difference is significant at 5% level.

Whereas all groups changed along this dimension, Methodists and Baptists did not differ from each other. Neither did the Baptists differ from the Church of Christ members, though the latter did differ from the Methodists. Church affiliation showed some differential effect on the changes on the A (acceptance of aggression) subscale of the POI (Table 21).

The final significant analysis in this connection was the effect of age on the changes in self-acceptance (Table 22). The youngest age group changed most, though the mean scores for this age group did not differ significantly from the mean score for the middle-aged group (i.e., forty to forty-three years old).

That the group members had known each other or were complete strangers did not seem to affect the changes manifested by the experimental group.

The POI data, on the whole, can be viewed to have supported the goals generally aimed by the sensitivity training movement. There was obviously sufficient change among the members of the experimental group to make a significant impact.

TABLE 22

The Effect of Age on the SA Subscale on the POI

Age	Pretest	Post Test	N	Mean	Difference (Pre-Post)
20 - 29	16.00	18.35	14	17.17	2.35*
30 - 39	14.07	15.33	13	14.80	1.46*
40 - 49	15.57	17.03	33	16.30	1.46*
50 - Up	14.56	16.20	48	15.38	1.64*

30 - 39, 50 - Up, 40 - 49, 20 - 29

Note: A line joining two numbers implies that the means were not different.

* Difference is significant at 5% level.

Factor Analysis

It has been mentioned earlier that the changes observed as a result of the administration of the POI took place immediately after the two-week training period. As compared to this, the changes observed on the basis of the ICL were evidenced between the first and the third testing, that is, were noticeable six months after training.

These results can be interpreted to imply that different kinds of behaviors are changed as a result of exposition to sensitivity training. In order to gain more definitive knowledge of these behaviors, it was decided to factor analyze the pretest scores of all the subscales of the POI and the ICL.

Thurstone's (1940, 1947) centroid method of factoring, using orthogonal rotations, was used. A twelve-factor solution

TABLE 23

Relevant Factor Loadings of POI and ICL

| Factor A | | Factor B | |
Variable	Loading	Variable	Loading
POI-I Scale	.81164	ICL-HI Scale	.59768
POI-Ex Scale	.72489	ICL-JK Scale	.73504
POI-Fr Scale	.70437	ICL-LM Scale	.63124
POI-Sa Scale	.54970	ICL-NO Scale	.59327
POI-A Scale	.61585		
POI-C Scale	.70150		
POI-O Scale	.80731		

| Factor C | | Factor D | |
Variable	Loading	Variable	Loading
POI-T_C Scale	.84151	ICL-AP Scale	.52055
POI-T_I Scale	.82331	POI-Sav Scale	.60042
		POI-Sr Scale	.55889
		POI-Sy Scale	.52078

*This Table gives factor loadings whose value is above .5.
Factor loadings less than .5 were not included.

was obtained. Table 23 lists the factor loadings of the four main factors obtained by this analysis. The rest of the factors obtained will not be listed here, as their factor loadings were very low and hence were considered unimportant.

The four factors reported in Table 22 can be interpreted as follows:

Factor A

It will be noticed that seven POI subscales had high loadings on this factor. It seemed that there is a common personality trait that is responsible for one's time competence, existentiality, feeling reactivity, self-acceptance, acceptance of aggression, capacity for intimate contact, and a healthy balance between inner directedness and other directedness as defined by Shostrom (1966). All the personality characteristics mentioned in this paragraph are attributes of self-actualization according to Shostrom; hence, Factor A might be called a factor of self-actualization. It seems that behavior that characterized this trait changed as a result of sensitivity training immediately after exposition to such a training.

Factor B

We notice that the ICL scales have high factor loadings on this scale. The HI scale has a loading of .59768, the JK scale has a loading of .73504, the LM scale has a loading of .63124, and the NO scale has a loading of .59327. According to the Interpersonal Diagnosis Multilevel Personality Pattern of Leary (1956), these subscales are close together in the circle describing the personality configuration. This factor can be interpreted by saying that there seems to be a common personality trait that is responsible for a person being self-effacing and masochistic and his being docile, dependent, and a clinging vine. Strangely enough, the same personality trait seems to be responsible for a person's being too cooperative and overconventional. It also is manifested in a person who spoils others with kindness, is too willing to give to others, and is overprotective of others and is generous to a fault. It seems that the kinds of behavior mentioned above are modified not immediately after sensitivity training (like Factor A), but a change in them is noticed after a lapse of time (i.e., approximately six months).

Factor C

It is evident from Table 22 that two subscales of the POI get high factor loadings on this factor, namely, T_C and T_I.

This factor can be interpreted by saying that the time ratio, as defined by Shostrom (page 15, 1966), is dependent on a personality trait that has little in common with the kinds of behaviors described under Factor A above. Since time ratio is quite important in the concept of self-actualization, it can be said that this factor represents another facet of self-actualization that is not related to Factor A. The kinds of behavior assessed by this factor are modified immediately after sensitivity training.

Factor D

ICL's AP subscale has a loading of .52055 on this factor, and we also notice that the POI SAV subscale has a factor loading of .60042; POI Sr subscale has a factor loading of .55889, and the POI Sy subscale has a factor loading of .52078.

It seems that there is a personality trait that is present in a person being managerial-autocratic; and the same trait seems to be responsible for a person's synergy, self-regard, and self-actualizing value. In other words, there seems to be a basic personality characteristic that operates in a person's being a good and forceful leader, and this characteristic seems to play a part in a person's ability to like oneself because of one's strength as a person and a person's ability to hold and live by values of self-actualizing people and his ability to see opposites of life as meaningfully related. Again this factor seems to be measuring another facet of self-actualization. Some of the behaviors assessed by this factor (subscales AP and Sr) seem to change as a result of sensitivity training after a lapse of time, as compared to Factor A, where behavior changes were noticed immediately after the end of training.

Semantic Differential

Osgood and his associates (1957) have argued convincingly through the years about the utility of the Semantic Differential Test developed by them. The flexibility of the test and its appropriateness in measuring some dimensions of an experimental nature suggested its suitability for the project. The three subscales of Evaluation, Potency, and Oriented Activity, suggested by the authors as the most reliable, were used to measure the psychological meaning of concepts that were considered to be directly related to the sensitivity training. The concepts chosen for measurement were the following:

a. Sensitivity training
b. Superior
c. Self
d. Relationship to others
e. Principal
f. Student
g. Trainer

TABLE 24

Comparison Between Experimental and
Control Groups on Total Amount of
Change on Semantic Differential Ratings

	Concept	Average Rank Experimental	Control	p
1.	Sensitivity Training	65	74	N.S.
2.	Superior	72	60	.04
3.	Self	71	62	N.S.
4.	Relationship to Others	69	66	N.S.
5.	Principal	69	65	N.S.
6.	Student	71	63	N.S.
7.	Trainer	67	70	N.S.

Two kinds of analyses were undertaken for the test: (1) an examination of the overall changes in the concepts and (2) changes in the concepts on the basis of the three subscales of Evaluation, Potency, and Oriented Activity.

The overall changes in the concepts from the Pretest to the Post-test 2 were not significant and did not differ for the experimental and control groups (Table 24). The only exception was the concept of superior, which changed differentially for the experimental group.

The second analysis related to the three subscales. Out of a total of twenty-one comparisons between the Pretest and Post-test 2 for each group, six were significant for the experimental group and one for the control group (Table 25). One of the most significant changes occurred in the concept of "self" on the Evaluative subscale. One may interpret this as an index of a heightened self-concept and one that is described among one of the goals of the training. Other significant changes for the

TABLE 25

Changes From Pretest to Post Test 2
in Semantic Differential Judgements
For Experimental and Control Groups

	Evaluation Exp. Cont.		Potency Exp. Cont.		Oriented Activity Exp. Cont.	
1. Sensitivity Training	N.S.	N.S.	N.S.	N.S.	N.S.	N.S.
2. Superior	N.S.	N.S.	.02	N.S.	.02	N.S.
3. Self	.001	N.S.	N.S.	N.S.	N.S.	N.S.
4. Relationship to Others	N.S.	N.S.	N.S.	N.S.	N.S.	N.S.
5. Principal	N.S.	N.S.	.04	N.S.	N.S.	N.S.
6. Student	N.S.	N.S.	N.S.	N.S.	N.S.	N.S.
7. Trainer	N.S.	.05	.02	N.S.	N.S.	N.S.

experimental group were for the concept of "superior" on both the Potency and Oriented Activity subscales. On the former scale, the experimental group changed significantly for both "Principle and Trainer."

The control group changed significantly only on the Evaluation subscale for trainer.

Motivational Analysis Test

Since sensitivity training presumes to work on relatively subtle factors of the personality, and the literature would lead one to believe that the primary influence will be on the person's motivation, it seems appropriate to obtain and analyze test and retest data from an objective instrument designed to measure motivation. The Motivation Analysis Test (Cattell, Horn, Sweeney, and Radcliffe, 1964) was administered for this purpose.

Since the Motivation Analysis Test (hereafter MAT) yields no less than twenty independent scores and a possible total of forty-five scores, if one includes those that are linearly dependent on the twenty basic ones, analysis of three sets of such data for each of a number of persons tends to maximize the chances that spurious results will be found unless careful steps are taken to counteract this. Analysis of data from any single score, or at least one score at a time, can expect to obtain significant results in some cases simply because of the sheer mass of data analyzed. One would expect, for example, analyzing by some simple t-test one factor at a time, to obtain approximately 5 percent of the results at the 5-percent confidence level. Obviously, what was required was some insurance against such spurious results, and fairly complex multivariate analyses were thus necessary.

The specific method utilized an analysis of covariants through the multiple regression model. The method is essentially standard and requires no description; however, it is desirable to emphasize one feature of the method, as follows:

An analysis with this model always begins by considering whether the total set of "independent variables" can produce a significant result in terms of the variance of the "dependent variable," which is explained or predicted. In other words, each analysis begins with the total set of scores, with appropriate shrinkage formulas and degrees of freedom to assure a nonsignificant result if that is a tenable hypothesis. If, and only if, the initial result is significant, then the model searches for those factors most clearly and dramatically related to the issue. If the total set of scores does not yield a highly significant result, then no further analysis is conducted.

Even within this model, however, a large number of analyses was made possible by the wealth of the data. One can compare, for example, both short-range (Post-test 1 minus Pretest 1) and long range (Post-test 2 minus Pretest 1) changes, not to mention changes that may result between the second and third testing. One can do this for experimentals separately from controls, for the total sample, for sexes and ages separately or together, and for breakdowns according to any other information that was available about the subjects. All such analyses were, in fact, performed, but reporting all of them will tend to bewilder the reader in a mass of statistical data that may serve to confuse and obscure rather than clarify the issue.

For that reason, the data presented here are those in which maximum clarity of results has been achieved. It should be stated, however, that all alternate methods of analyses yielded equally significant or insignificant results, as the case may be, in a completely consistent and logical pattern. The results here described are not attributable to chance by any reasonable stretch of the imagination.

Let us begin the analysis by considering short-range changes as they can be contrasted between the experimental and control groups. Table 26 shows analyses of change scores in which, for convenience of applying the model, the changes in motivational scores were considered to be the "independent variables" or "predictors," while membership in either the experimental or the control group was considered the "dependent variable" or "criterion." In other words, the questions were asked, to what extent is it possible to determine whether a person belongs to the experimental or the control group from

TABLE 26

Short Range Changes — (Test 2 — Test 1)

Experimental Vs. Control

M.A.T.-Factor	DF_1	DF_2	F-Ratio	Sig.	Type of Change
Overall:	20	159	2.69	< .001	
Career-U	9	170	10.00	< .001	Exper. decrease in (U I) career > controls
I	9	170	5.71	< .001	
Fear-U	9	170	2.23	< .05	Exper. decrease in (U) fear > controls
S.E.-U	9	170	10.16	< .001	Exper. decrease in (U) Superego > controls
S.S.-U	9	170	2.40	< .05	Exper. decrease in (U) Self-sentiment;controls increase
Narc.-I	9	170	5.56	< .001	Exper. increase in (I) narcism; controls decrease
S.S.-I	9	170	6.77	< .001	Exper. increase in (I) Self-sentiment > controls
Pug.-I	9	170	2.77	< .01	Exper. decrease in (I) pugnacity; controls increase
Ass.-I	9	170	4.21	< .001	Controls increase in (I) assertiveness > exper.

an inspection only of the change scores in these motivational patterns between the time of Pretest and the reassessment of Post-test 2.

The overall significance of the comparison is clearly expressed by an F-ratio of 2.69 which, with 20 and 159 degrees of freedom, respectively, yields a significant result beyond the .001 level. Clearly, something happened to the experimental subjects that was different from what happened to the controls.

While the fact that the observed changes conform to the literature of expectations regarding the sensitivity training experiences, it cannot be taken as evidence of validity; however, the data do match such expectations rather well. If sensitivity training encourages a more comfortable and less inhibited and rigid life style, then the finding that motivation toward career success, both at unintegrated and at integrated levels, decreases among those undergoing the experience, and that this happens more in these experimental subjects than in the controls, must be considered as confirming the expectations. If sensitivity training should produce reductions in fear, then the finding that this takes place should be considered sensible. If the rigidity of superego structures and of concern for reputation are decreased by the experience, then the finding of such change is again sensible. If sensitivity training tends to result in an increase in what some psychotherapists would describe as healthy selfishness, then the data regarding narcissism are sensible. If self-acceptance is enhanced by those group experiences, then the increase in integrated self-sentiment, coupled with the decrease in unintegrated concern in this area, is to be expected. If those groups help people resolve tensions, then the decrease in pugnacity and generalized nastiness among the experimental subjects, with a corresponding increase of such pugnacity among the controls, must be considered in the expected direction. Finally, if assertiveness is strongly related to pugnacity, as is the case in the Motivation Analysis Test, then the last finding in the table also is sensible.

As stated above, "sensibleness" is not proof. However, when attention is paid to the degree to which the changes shown in Table 26 match those that a reasonable sensitivity

72

training group leader would expect, and since these changes are clearly of substantial significance, they seem to constitute definitive proof that some significant changes in the person are associated with the experience, changes that do not take place in a comparable group experience of a different type.

A second issue concerns the question of short-range versus long-range changes. Table 27 shows these changes as they relate to preexisting conditions of the subject. That short-range changes would be somewhat different from long-range changes, assuming that change occurs at all, is not surprising. One would

TABLE 27

Short Range Vs. Long Range Changes (MAT)

Experimental only: Changes Related to Pre-existing Condition

Condition	Short/Long	DF_1	DF_2	F-Ratio	Sig
Sex	S	20	104	.63	n.s.
	L	20	93	1.52	n.s.
Marital Status	S	20	104	1.22	n.s.
	L	20	93	1.11	n.s.
Age	S	20	104	.77	n.s.
	L	20	93	2.27	<.01
Prof. Exper.	S	20	104	.85	n.s.
	L	20	93	2.41	<.01
Income	S	20	104	.83	n.s.
	L	20	93	.89	n.s.
Church*	S	20	104	1.14	n.s.
	L	20	93	1.03	n.s.
Type Group	S	20	104	1.26	n.s.
	L	20	93	1.46	n.s.

* Liberalism Vs. Fundamentalism of Affiliation

expect, however, that any differences along these lines would relate to preexisting conditons, and it is logical to believe that such relatively unchanging conditions as sex, age, professional experience, etc., if related at all to change, would be more strongly related to long-range than to short-range changes. That is exactly the case.

In Table 27, changes as related to the preexisting conditions were analyzed separately for short-range and long-range patterns. The most surprising finding in the entire table is the relative insignificance of these preexisting conditions as they are associated with the changes that take place in the experimental group. However, age and professional experience, which are, to some extent, measures of similar things, do relate clearly to long-range changes and not to short-range ones. The finding, amplified below, that, in general, young people and inexperienced people show greater change in the long run than do their elder and more experienced peers is completely consistent with both an intuitive expectation and the data available in the literature.

A further word about the absence of relationship seems appropriate. The experimental subjects show profound change in their motivations, but that change is not associated with whether they are male or female, with their marital status, with their income, with the type of church they belong to, and, interestingly enough, with the type of the training group in which they participated. The last of these approaches significance most closely, but, in general, this would seem to be evidence to support the contention of the sensitivity training leaders that the experience of such a group is likely to influence participants regardless of preexisting conditions.

Let us turn next to the analysis of the long-range experimental group changes that were shown in Table 26 and are given in detail in Tables 28 and 29.

Long-range changes in experimental subjects as these relate to the age of the subject, suggest that the person's stability is influenced by his age and that younger subjects have greater capacity to show changes than do older ones. Specifically, the

TABLE 28

Long Range Experimental Group Changes
As Related to Age

MAT-Factor	DF_1	DF_2	F-Ratio	Sig.	Type of Change
U - War	6	107	8.63	< .001	Older members do not increase in (U) Narcissism as much as young
U - S.S.	6	107	8.01	< .001	Younger members decrease in (U) Self-sentiment, older do not
U - Sex	6	107	3.18	< .01	Younger increase (U) mating > older
U - Pug	6	107	5.11	< .001	Pugnacity (U) increases more in older than in younger
I - Parent	6	107	10.62	< .001	(I) ties to parents decrease among older > younger
I - Sex	6	107	2.98	< .05	(I) Same as (U) Sex above

TABLE 29

Long Range Experimental Group Changes
As Related to Teaching Experience

MAT-Factor	DF_1	DF_2	F-Ratio	Sig.	Type of Change
U – Car	9	104	7.74	< .01	(U) Career decrease greatest among most experienced
U – Nar	9	104	8.51	< .001	(U) Narcism increase least among most Narcissim experienced
U – S.S.	9	104	4.19	< .001	(U) Self-sentiment decrease least among most experienced
U & I – Sex	9 9	104 104	3.82 2.89	< .001 < .01	(U & I) mating increase least among most experienced (older?)
U – Pug	9	104	8.17	< .001	(U) Pugnacity increase greatest among most experienced
I – Par	9	104	8.25	< .001	Decrease in (I) ties to parents greatest among most experienced
I – Fear	9	104	2.21	< .05	(I) Fear decrease greatest in most experienced
I – Ass	9	104	2.22	< .05	(I) Assertiveness increases among experienced, decreases among newer

76

selfishness and narcissism that tends to be a result of most psychotherapeutic experiences occurs primarily among the younger experimental subjects. Concern about self-sentiment and reputation in the community decreases among younger members of the experimental groups but not among the older. Sexual drive, both unintegrated and integrated, increases among the young more than among the old. Pugnacity, an expression of aggressiveness in response to frustrating circumstances, is the only one of the characteristics in which the change among older people is greater than among younger ones. One may hypothesize that the impetus to change in a sensitivity training experience could be more frustrating to the older person and that this, in turn, may produce some feelings of frustration and resulting aggressiveness. Finally, if one interprets a loosening of ties to the parents as a type of maturity, and the MAT findings available suggest that this is a reasonable interpretation, then it would be appropriate for such change to take place to a greater extent among the older than among the younger group members, and that is a finding.

Again, the sensibleness of the results in Table 28 is not evidence. The extremely high significance of these findings, coupled with the fact that the findings are at least minimally reasonable, can be interpreted as further evidence of significant change as a result of the sensitivity training experience.

Long-range changes as related to professional experience are documented in Table 29. To some extent, professional experience and age are alternate ways of describing the same thing, but this is only partly the case. The pattern in Table 29 is quite similar to that in Table 28, but some significant exceptions seem more to relate to experience than to age as such.

One will note that the findings in Table 29 regarding narcissism, self-sentiment, sex, pugnacity, and ties to the parents duplicate the findings in Table 28. In addition, there are three types of changes that occur most heavily among the most experienced group members, a decrease in unintegrated career motivation, a decrease in fear, and an increase in assertiveness. These findings could be considered logical and sensible but not to the overwhelming degree that was present in the other tables. Rather, the findings are of substantial statistical significance and seem worthy of further exploration.

A notable fact is that, when comparing Table 29 with Table 28, the most significant results in each are the same, whereas the three types of change that appear in Table 28 alone do not reach quite the extreme level of significance shown in the other scores. These clearly are changes of smaller magnitude.

Summary

The above pages clearly demonstrate that, overall, the group of educators experienced significant changes during the course of the sensitivity training. These changes were demonstrated, to lesser or greater degree, in all the tests utilized in the assessment of the internal criteria. The sensitivity training literature suggests that the changes are both obvious and immediate and subtle and long term. Our findings confirmed both kinds of changes. The experimental group, as compared to the control group, verbalized through the tests changes that were experienced immediately after the training and those that were manifest six months later.

Our data also generated a wealth of hypotheses that must await further corroboration.

Chapter IV

EXTERNAL CRITERIA

The previous chapter has made it clear that the educators who went through the sensitivity training felt that they had changed. All the measures were self-report measures. In order to assess how far their self-perception generated changes in their relationships with others, samples from two populations that had direct contact with them were tapped, namely, the principals of the schools where they worked and the students that came in contact with them.

The most relevant relationship of educators is with the student who comes in contact with them. Two sets of measures were used to tap the perceptions of the students, one a projective measure that aimed at measuring some of the covert level and, second, the ICL, which had been used as a measure of the internal criteria and was intended as a measure of an overt level. The results from the assessment of the students' perception will be described first and then the responses of the principals.

The Picture Test

The test consisted of six pictures, five of these chosen from the Michigan Picture Test (Hartwell, Hutt, and Walton, 1953) and one from the Thematic Apperception Test (Murray, 1943). The first picture depicted a classroom scene of a boy standing next to the teacher's desk with the teacher in her chair and other children in the classroom. The second picture depicted a boy standing beside a desk behind which an older man sat. The third picture depicted a girl sitting alone in an otherwise vacant classroom. The fourth picture depicted four figures in the middle of the road supposedly walking down that road. A fifth picture was that of a streak of lightning in the sky during the dark night with house lights and other clues of a town. The last picture was a blank card from the Thematic Apperception Test. The instructions given were those used for the Thematic Apperception Test, namely, that the students had to write stories centering around the pictures and state the present, the past, the future, and the feelings of the characters in the story. The stories were anonymously written except for age, sex, and grade. Two groups of students were tested. The experimental group consisted of sixty students who had been taught by teachers who had been through the sensitivity training. The control group consisted of fifty students who had been taught by teachers who had not participated in the training sessions.

The experimental group had thirty-two males and twenty-eight females, between seventeen and twenty years of age in the eleventh and twelfth grades. The control group had twenty-two males and twenty females, also seventeen to twenty years of age and in the twelfth grade. The students came from similar socioeconomic backgrounds and from school districts that were regarded as constituting similar groups in terms of most major dimensions.

The responses to these cards were examined in order to get an assessment of the students' attitudes toward the school situation as such. More specifically, assessment was made of the students' perception of themselves in their interaction with their teachers, their perception of the teachers, their general attitude toward the school, and their attitudes toward their own role within the context of the school situation. It was felt that the blank card mentioned above gave indication of the general attitude of the student toward the school, their teacher, the testing situation, and was symbolic of the student's overall reaction to their general role as a student. Most of these assessments will be discussed below.

TABLE 30

Perception of Self
(Picture Test)

	Experimental				Control			
	Male	Female	Total	%	Male	Female	Total	%
Positive (Student Role & Adequacy)	18	24	42	70%	6	10	16	32%
Done something wrong (guilty); will correct	20	21	41	68%	4	9	13	26%
Feeling bad; scared; self-depreciatory remarks	17	7	24	40%	11	20	31	62%
Deviant behavior	26	26	52	87%	19	28	47	94%
"Laying out" Revengeful & angry at teacher	10	6	16	27%	15	25	40	80%
Future bad or uncertain	4	2	6	10%	7	11	18	36%
Future good or better	7	17	24	40%	6	10	16	32%

In almost all cases, the first four cards brought forth themes related to school life. The last two cards sometimes did the same thing indirectly. The contents of the themes presented were analyzed and a frequency count made of the number of times a theme was expressed as an indication of the student's perception of his own role. As Table 30 indicates, there is a marked difference between the two groups. Whereas 70 percent of the experimental group perceived the student's role as being positive, only 32 percent of the control group did so. The former implied that the students saw themselves as learning, trying to understand, expressing some sense of adequacy as well as a sense of importance about what they did. These responses ranged from the student's perception of indulging in activities of learning, etc., to an expression of their own adequacy and wish to improve themselves. Card III, depicting the adult man with a smaller child, was almost invariably seen as a case of some deviant behavior on the child's part. Both the control and the experimental groups tended to perceive this as a case of a child faced with having violated some rule of the school. The difference is marked in the reaction of the students to the situation and gave an indication of how they dealt with it; 68 percent of the experimental group felt that the hero had done something wrong but that the future would bring forth a correction of this misdeed usually through punishment or related methods used by the authority concerned. As compared with this, only 26 percent of the control group expressed such sentiments. In these same themes, the respondents expressed feelings of being scared or made some kind of a self-deprecatory remark. Here the differences are not as marked but still continue to be present; 40 percent of the experimental group and 62 percent of the control group expressed these feelings. The theme of deviant behavior was perceived by 87 percent of the experimental group and 94 percent of the control group. Several students expressed the idea of either playing "hooky" or feeling revengeful, resentful, and angry at the teacher. The differences, here again, are in the predicted direction, so that 27 percent of the experimental group and 80 percent of the control group feel that such a solution is the best adjustment. The intensity of the children's negative feelings in this context are quite obvious. For the control group, it took strong forms such as "hits the teacher, will get even with her someday," "the boy has been unjustly sent to the principal," "the cat (the boy) in the leather jacket may at any moment pull a knife on the guy with the tie (teacher)," or "these children are mad at their teacher," and for the experimental group examples were of "the child's feelings are anger at her teacher," "some kid beat the heck out of her teacher," and "the boy probably tells the teacher he was a nasty old man." In spite of the specific test directions, every student did not make a statement about the future, only some did so. Here again, the differences hold up, though they are not as marked as the above-mentioned dimensions. Thirty-six percent of the control group felt that their future was bad or uncertain, whereas only 10 percent of the experimental group said so. As opposed to this, 40 percent of the experimental group mentioned that their future was either good or would be better, and only 32 percent of the controls said the same thing.

Linked closely with the student's perception of his own role in this context was an assessment of a general attitude of how helpless or effective a student feels. This attitude does not give the content, that is, the helplessness is not necessarily an indication of complete compliance, nor is a sense of effectiveness an indication of very positive attitudes. The attitude refers to the degree to which the student felt that he could do something about his situation or felt that he was completely at the mercy of the forces around him. The students' responses were rated along a five-point scale, ranging from the extremely internally oriented to an extremely external orientation.* Neither end of the five-point scale, namely, the completely internal orientation nor the completely external orientation, were present frequently. In fact, only two of the students from the experimental group expressed an extremely internal orientation. These were, therefore, regarded as part of a tendency toward an internal orientation. The other categories were a mixed orientation and a tendency toward an external orientation. The last category, namely, an extremely external orientation, was dropped from the statistical analysis since none of the respondents could be classified as such. A chi square was significant at more that the .02 level. The experimental group, as the data

---

*Since this research was carried out, the locus of control variable, as described by Rotter (1960), has been heavily researched.

(Table 31) shows, tends to be more internally oriented and the control group more externally oriented. There seemed to be no difference in the groups as far as the mixed orientation, namely, neither internal or external orientation, was concerned. A look at the responses suggested that some of the internal orientation also involved negative attitudes toward the teacher, where the student felt that he would get even with the teacher or that he could do something to irritate her. This was more prominent in the control group than in the experimental group. As Rotter (1966) has pointed out, the importance of this attitude in the general adjustment of a person in his life is extremely important. It may well be assumed that those students who feel completely at the mercy of the social forces surrounding them, namely, the school situation, are more liable to have difficulty in making affective adjustment toward life. As has been mentioned above, some of the internally oriented responses indicate antisocial behavior that is very likely to lead the student into conflict with the social forces later on, but it is apparent that if a person feels extremely helpless, there is very little he is liable to do since he does not see himself as emanating any effective measures on his own.

TABLE 31

Internal - External Orientation
(Picture Test)

	Experimental	Control	Total
Internal	28	11	39
Neither Internal or External	15	14	29
External	17	25	42
Total	60	50	110

$x^2 = 8.07$

p .02

The next major dimension for which the responses were assessed was the perception of the teacher. The positive perception involved seeing the teacher as a source of identification where she was fulfilling her chief function of being a teacher and was helpful, understanding, and supportive. A negative perception consisted of such themes as the teacher being inadequate, boring, or extremely punishing. A glance at Table 32 will show that 65 percent of the experimental group and only 30 percent of the control group expressed positive feelings toward their teachers. As far as the negative sentiments were concerned, there were again very marked differences in the perceptions of the two groups; 43 percent of the experimental group and 92 percent of the control group saw the teacher as punishing, as unjustly punitive or unfair. Some of these perceptions also involved seeing the teacher as inadequate and boring in person. Card II invariably brought forth the theme of the principal talking to a student. Less than ten respondents saw the older person in the picture as representing either an uncle, a warden, or some other authority figure. The responses of the majority were again sorted into positive or negative remarks about the principal. The experimental group had more or less the same amount of the two kinds of responses in the two categories, that is, 38 percent of their remarks were positive and 42 percent were negative (Table 33). In contrast with this, the control group showed a marked preference for negative remarks toward the principal, so that 66 percent of the group saw the principal as being extremely negative, and only 22 percent saw the principal as being positive. The positive remarks about the principal expressed a conviction that he must punish the child for the child's own future good or that the principal was a source of a gratifying identification in some other way. At times, this was brought forth in the theme of the principal trying to help the child see right from wrong or in generally counseling him for his own good. The negative remarks consisted of the principal being "mad, unfair, and extremely punitive."

Not every student made direct references to the school. The result is that we do not have responses of every child on

TABLE 32

Perception of Teacher
(Picture Test)

| Teacher | Experimental | | | | Control | | | |
	Male	Female	Total	%	Male	Female	Total	%
Positive	20	19	39	65%	3	12	15	30%
Negative	18	8	26	43%	23	23	46	92%

TABLE 33

Perception of Principal
(Picture Test)

| Principal | Experimental | | | | Control | | | |
	Male	Female	Total	%	Male	Female	Total	%
Positive	12	11	23	38%	2	9	11	22%
Negative	12	13	25	42%	17	16	33	66%

a direct expression of their sentiments about school but only in some cases. Here again, there is a marked difference between the two groups; 10 percent of the experimental and only 2 percent of the control expressed pleasant sentiments toward the schools and saw this as a worthwhile experience (Table 34). In comparison with this, 18 percent of the experimental and 32 percent of the control saw the school as something to be avoided and as generally a very unpleasant part of their life.

The last dimension to be studied was the student's reac-

TABLE 34

Perception of the School
(Picture Test)

School	Experimental				Control			
	Male	Female	Total	%	Male	Female	Total	%
Pleasant	3	3	6	10%	0	1	1	2%
Unpleasant	5	6	11	18%	8	8	16	32%

tions to the blank card mentioned above. Since the card asked for the student to make a story of his own, it brought forth a range of responses that were regarded as symbolic expressions of their general attitude of their own role within the school situation. The responses ranged from extreme hostility toward the examiner to an expression of the bright future that lay ahead for the students as they left the school. It was felt that the positive responses in this case were a combination of the student's perception of his role within the school situation, his general attitude about how effective his own behavior could be in shaping his life, as well as his general reaction to the teacher's role and other adult figures. Some of the students gave no response to the card; however, they made some remarks so that their statement could be divided into a positive statement, a negative statement or a neutral statement. The positive remarks stated that they could not see anything, but they generally had a good feeling about the card; the negative remarks stated that they saw nothing in the picture and made some hostile comment about being asked to do such a "stupid" thing. The neutral category consisted of remarks where the student gave no indication of his feelings about the card either positive or negative. Some of the respondents proceeded to see something that ranged from a symbolic expression of their own future to a concrete picture. These could also be classified as being generally positive, negative, or neutral. Both sets of responses to the blank card were combined and a chi square computed for differences between the experimental and control groups. A look at Table 35 will show that the chi^2 for differences between these categories is 24.43 and for this size sample is significant at beyond the .001 level. A look at the data shows that here again differences come from the positive and negative categories rather than the neutral one. The differences again appear to be in the predicted directions, so that the experimental group tends to give more positive remarks as opposed to the control and fewer negative remarks as opposed to the control. The highest frequency is that of the negative remarks made by the control group.

TABLE 35

Response to Card VI
(Blank Card)

	Experimental	Control	Total
Positive	25	6	31
Negative	9	29	38
Neutral	26	15	41
Total	60	50	

$x^2 = 24.43$

p   .001

In summary, then, it is apparent that the students do not form dichotomous groups. They do tend to see themselves as being involved in deviant behaviors and perceive themselves as being in the wrong within the school context. It seems that both groups, when shown the picture where the child is facing an adult, tended to see deviant acts and that the child had done something wrong. Since the test was given in a school situation, it had all the associations of the school attached to it. The interesting comment to be made, however, here is that the interactions with the teacher do bring forth either completely negative or constructive responses to these situations. It can, therefore, be stated that obviously the teachers who had been through the sensitivity training bring forth, in at least some of the students, a sense of identification with themselves as well as a sense of constructive action being available to the students within the total school situation. Since these were high school students who were at the threshold of graduation, it may logically be assumed that their attitudes toward their teachers and the school were bound to affect their attitude toward the general adult society that they entered fully after their graduation. It was also apparent that it cannot be logically assumed that the control group consisted of students only with negative reactions but that the teachers in these situations apparently failed to bring forth a positive interaction between themselves and the students.

It was apparent that if a student had been interacting with a teacher who had been through the training, he or she was more likely to be involved with such activities as learning, studying, preparing for the future, to feel a sense of identity with the teacher whose punishing activities he or she perceived as being for his or her own good, to see the future to be good, and to see his own actions to some extent being determined by himself or herself than if he or she got a teacher who had not had such training. The student may still have managed to arrive at the same point, as indeed some did, but, apparently, the interactions with the school environment tended to reduce the possibility of their being able to do so.

Students' Ratings of Teachers

The two groups of students were asked to complete the ICL for themselves and for their teachers. The preliminary result of this comparison is presented below.

No significant differences were found between the two groups of students when their ratings of themselves were compared. This analysis, summarized in Table 36, was performed to ensure that the two groups of raters were comparable. This allowed any differences in the ratings of the teachers to be more likely related to the teachers' behavior than to biases in the samples of students.

TABLE 36

Students' Ratings of Themselves
on the Interpersonal Check List
Means and Significance Tests

Scale		Experimental Group	Control Group	Significance
AP	Mean	4.68	3.84	NS
	Variance	5.32	6.49	
BC	Mean	4.92	4.47	NS
	Variance	4.46	5.54	
DE	Mean	4.41	4.20	NS
	Variance	4.47	6.59	
FG	Mean	4.98	4.92	NS
	Variance	6.30	9.99	
HI	Mean	5.06	5.20	NS
	Variance	7.05	7.18	
JK	Mean	5.51	5.59	NS
	Variance	9.36	9.03	
LM	Mean	7.35	7.12	NS
	Variance	9.85	8.26	
NO	Mean	5.03	5.00	NS
		10.28	11.33	

By inspection, it can easily be seen that these students had a very uncomplimentary view of teachers in general, whether they were the teachers who had been through sensitivity training or not. When the student raters' view of their teachers is compared with those teachers' view of themselves, gross discrepancies appear. The students seem to have in general a picture of teachers as hostile, authoritarian, rigid people with few of the saving graces of concern for others, love, or modesty. This cultural stereotype (perhaps only an exaggeration of any adolescent's view of an adult authority figure) seemed to pervade the ratings and to overpower the discrimination power of any given scale since no significant differences were found between the rating of the teachers by either group (Table 37).

TABLE 37

Students' Ratings of Teachers on
the Interpersonal Check List
Means and Significance Tests

| Scale | Teacher Ratings | | |
		Experimental Group	Control Group	Significance
AP	Mean	8.16	8.61	NS
	Variance	5.91	7.49	
BC	Mean	7.38	8.10	NS
	Variance	7.33	8.56	
DE	Mean	7.56	8.20	NS
	Variance	6.79	6.94	
FG	Mean	6.19	6.96	NS
	Variance	11.81	13.49	
HI	Mean	3.10	2.43	NS
	Variance	6.28	3.78	
JK	Mean	4.52	3.67	NS
	Variance	8.53	5.67	
LM	Mean	4.87	4.13	NS
	Variance	13.70	12.48	
NO	Mean	4.29	3.59	NS
		10.61	7.07	

However, close inspection of the mean ratings of the groups on the eight subscales showed that on the four more negative scales, the control group had higher scores, and on the four more positive scales, the experimental group had higher means. This observation was in the expected direction and was followed up by an analysis of the two groups, using combined scores of what Leary (1958) calls Dominance (Dom) and Love (Lov), derived from a differential weighting and combination of the various positive and negative subscales. This analysis is summarized in Table 38.

TABLE 38

Students' Ratings of Teachers:
Dominance (DOM) and Love (LOV) Scores,**
Means and Significance Tests

	Experimental Group	Control Group	Significance*
Love (LOV)			
Mean	-5.79	-9.52	p < .025
Variance	82.83	110.19	
Dominance (DOM)			
Mean	5.73	6.92	p = .05
Variance	14.12	13.85	

* A one-tailed significance test was employed on both scores with the rationale that the experimental group would be higher on LOV and lower on DOM, which was confirmed.

** DOM = 0.7 (BC+NO-FG-JK) + AP-HI

LOV = 0.7 (JK+NO-BC-FG) + LM-DE

As can be seen from the analysis, the results are statistically significant and indicate that the teachers in the experimental group are seen as less hostile and more accepting than the control-group teachers. This confirms the tendency noted in the initial analysis, although the levels of the scores still indicate a very unflattering picture of teachers in general when viewed by their students. In any case, it can be surmised that teachers who had been exposed to sensitivity training seemed to relate in a more positive manner to the students as compared to teachers who had not been exposed to such training. This data confirmed the findings of the previous section. However, it seems that the Picture Test, apparently because of its disguised aim, led the experimental students to express much more positive attitudes toward themselves and their teachers as well as the school situation then they did on ICL.

Ratings by Principals

The second population tapped to get a measure of the external criteria were the school principals of the teachers, both in the experimental and the control group. Ryan's Characteristics of Teacher's Rating Scale (1960) was used to get the ratings.

In application, the Characteristics of Teacher's Rating Scale resulted in difficulties as far as the statistical analysis was concerned. Designed as a forced-choice instrument in which the

TABLE 39

Principals' Ratings of
Teachers Characteristics

	Experimental Group	Significance of Differences	Control Group
No.	107		55
No. Positive Statements	Mean - 19.36 S.D. - 5.49	NS $p < .10$	16.96 6.56
No. Negative Statements	Mean - 2.20 S.D. - 3.18	NS	2.42 4.10
No. Blank Items	Mean - 3.39 S.D. - 4.29	$p < .01$	5.66 4.28

rater was to check either a positive or negative statement about the teacher being rated, the results showed that the raters were extremely reluctant to check the negative items of the scale and left many items blank. This caused the analysis to be somewhat indirect in that all subjects were not rated on exactly the same number of items. For the positive statements, the difference between the experimental and control groups was not statistically significant. However, there was a tendency for the teachers exposed to the sensitivity training to be viewed positively by the principals. There was no difference between the experimental and control groups so far as the negative statements were concerned. A significant difference (p less than .01) was found in the number of blanks per questionnaire, with the experimental group receiving fewer blank ratings. Table 39 gives details of this analysis.

These results may have resulted from several sources, for example, a bias of the raters in favor of teachers known to have been in a training program or, on the other hand, a greater ease in rating the experimental group.

An additional analysis of the results, accounting for the unequal numbers of items for each subject, was performed by analyzing the results item by item in terms of which group and the higher percentage of members checked positively for a given item. This analysis showed that on twenty of the twenty-five items, a higher percentage of the experimental group was checked positively. Table 40 gives details of this analysis. This difference was found statistically significant (p less than .001), using the Sign Test (Siegal, 1956), suggesting that indeed the experimental group as a whole was rated more favorably by their immediate supervisors.

The implication of these findings seems to be that teachers exposed to sensitivity training are viewed more positively by their principals and supervisors.

Summary

An effort was made to assess the effects of sensitivity train-

TABLE 40

Item Analysis of Principals Rating
of Teachers, Per Cents of Teachers
Receiving Positive Ratings

Item	Experimental Group Per Cent Positive	Control Group Per Cent Positive	Sign of Diff
1	83	82	+
2	94	82	+
3	80	60	+
4	72	78	−
5	73	53	+
6	64	49	+
7	87	93	−
8	83	78	+
9	84	84	0
10	90	87	+
11	76	76	0
12	85	69	+
13	81	71	+
14	52	58	−
15	91	84	+
16	67	56	+
17	79	44	+
18	73	53	+
19	73	45	+
20	69	49	+
21	76	67	+
22	71	55	+
23	75	69	+
24	89	85	+
25	68	65	+

Sign test 20+,
3−, $p < .001$

ing on educators. This evaluation utilized internal and external criteria and matched control groups. Internal criteria were measured by the F Scale, the Personal Orientation Inventory, Semantic Differential, ICL, and the Motivation Analysis Test. External criteria were assessed by ICL, a Picture Test, and Ryan's Rating Scale.

Effects of the training were studied by examining changes along each of these measures. The implications of the results were discussed in detail.

It seems that educators exposed to sensitivity training became less authoritarian and more self-actualized. They developed better interpersonal relationships in addition to developing greater self-insight and leadership skills.

A factor analysis was attempted to explain differential changes in behavior over a period of time. Four major factors were described in detail in this context. An effort was made to study the importance of variables, for example, marital status, years of teaching experience, church affiliation, etc., on sensitivity training. The relevant importance of each of these in terms of the different measures was described. An attempt was made to predict changes as a result of the training on the basis of prediction equations.

Educators exposed to the training were perceived more positively by their supervisors as well as by their students. Students' perceptions of their teachers were described in detail.

It can be safely concluded that sensitivity training can play a crucial role in the training of educators and thereby in the process of education. Not only does such training help them as persons, but it seems that this improvement in their selves is reflected in a positive manner in their external environment, namely, the schools. One might hazard a guess that if all our educators could be exposed to such training at periodic time intervals, the whole process of education would function more efficiently and smoothly.

SECTION TWO

Chapter V

ASSESSMENT OF THE
THIRD-YEAR PARTICIPANTS

The preceding section has dealt with the assessment of the effects of sensitivity training program on the participants of the Upper Cumberland Project during the second year. This section will deal with the assessment during the third year.

The sample in the third year consisted of seventy-one educators, all of whom had participated in the training program either during 1968 or 1969. The selection of the sample was made by the training staff who had worked with these participants in consultation with the director and the codirector of the project. The results of the assessment of the second year could not be used as a basis for the selection since the data analysis was not complete by the time the participants had to be chosen.

In the clinical judgment of the staff, these participants had shown potential to become effective change agents in their respective communities. The goal was not that the participants become trainers in their own right but that they could assist other leaders in the future. It was hoped that the various school systems would incorporate, on a regular basis, some sensitivity training in their inservice programs.

The participants ranged in age from twenty-one to sixty-one years, with a mean age of 45.8 years. Fifty-one percent were males and 49 percent females. They included elementary to high school teachers and some administrators. As in the previous years, the participants were paid fifteen dollars for each day they attended in addition to three dollars per day for each dependent.

The assessment consisted of two parts: (1) a feedback questionnaire and (2) an open-ended interview. Because of practical limitations, the second part of the assessment was limited to twenty of the participants. A comparable group of twenty persons was also selected and interviewed.

The twenty persons who comprised the experimental group for the interviews were chosen in a random stratified manner from the total number of participants. The strata used in the sample selection were the density of population, the participating counties, the nature of jobs, and the kinds of schools from which they came. An effort was made to have an even number of males and females.

In order to select a control group, each participant in the program was asked to nominate two individuals who were similar in terms of their age, occupation, and number of years of teaching experiences to himself or herself and who had not participated in the program. Half of the control group consisted of a random sample from these nominations, taking care that one person was selected at least for each participant. The other half of the control group was chosen from a school system that had not been exposed to the sensitivity training during the three years, in order to maximize the inclusion of those who would know very little or not at all about the program.

Participants in the control group were paid ten dollars for each interview.

A statistical analysis of the ages, income, and the number of dependents of the experimental and control groups indicated that the two groups did not differ significantly.

In the first two years of the project, the sensitivity training had extended over a two-week period. The third-year training lasted for three weeks. The first week was devoted to programmed problem-solving exercises, named the RUPS model (Jung and Lippitt, 1966). The second week was devoted to self-examination and planning for the future through concentration of the main dimensions described in Appendix D. The third week was devoted to a discussion of "back home" problems in the school systems and their possible solutions. This involved interpersonal interactions among persons who held similar jobs. This was followed by interactions among different school faculties, which, in turn, were followed by school systems in a county interchanging and discussing problems. Lastly, the different counties made an attempt to arrive at a solution of some of their problems.

The Assessment Measures

The main consideration in the choice of the assessment measures during this period were (1) those that had not been included in the previous year and (2) their feasibility in view of the great reduction in the size of the program. As mentioned above, the measures consisted of a feedback questionnaire and an open-ended interview. The results are presented below for each of them.

Feedback Questionnaire

A questionnaire consisting of fourteen items was administered anonymously to the participants at the end of the workshop with the intention of finding details about their reactions to the experience. A copy of the questionnaire is reproduced in Appendix E. It was designed to get global reactions as well as reactions to specific techniques used in the workshop. These techniques are commonly a part of one form or another of sensitivity training.

Some of the questions could be answered in a "yes," "no," and "don't know" fashion. These responses were classified into mutually exclusive categories. However, other questions, namely, numbers 1, 7, 11, 13(a), and 14 were more open-ended. These responses were classified into several categories that were neither mutually exclusive nor comprehensive. Consequently, some answers were classified as falling into more than one category (Tables 41–56). The percentage in these questions are

TABLE 41

Q 1: Did the workshop meet your expectations?

	No.	%
Yes	64	94%
Yes and No	3	3%
No	1	1%

an indication of how many of the total number of respondents expressed that sentiment rather than a percentage of all the sentiments expressed. In all cases, the percentages were rounded off.

The first question asked was whether the workshop met the expectations of the participants. Ninety-four percent of the respondents stated that it did so, 4 percent gave a qualified yes, and only one individual stated that it did not meet his expectations. The people who reported that the workshop did meet their expectations wholly or partially gave some details of what they meant.

A look at Table 42 shows that 29 percent of the respondents stated that they felt that their understanding of themselves was better. Another 29 percent felt that their relationships with other people were better. Nine percent felt that their ability to communicate was better. Seven percent felt that they were able to solve their problems more adequately. Some of the respondents did not talk directly about themselves but in their responses talked more of their participation as a group member. Ten percent of these felt that all of them understood each other better. Twenty-five percent felt that the experience was relevant to their jobs. Ten percent felt that the useful things were some specific techniques that they acquired during the experience.

TABLE 42

Q 1: Ways in which workshop met expectations

	No.	%
Emphasis on self		
1. "My understanding of self is better."	20	29%
2. "My understanding of relationships with others is better."	20	29%
3. "My ability to communicate is better."	6	9%
4. "My ability to solve problems is better."	5	7%
Emphasis on group		
5. "All of us understand each other better."	7	10%
6. "We aired our problems."	1	1%
7. "We met new people."	1	1%
Emphasis on workshop		
8. "Workshop was relevant to my job."	17	25%
9. "Workshop was relevant to student-teacher relationships."	1	1%
10. "Workshop offered good techniques."	7	10%
11. "Workshop staff was good."	5	7%
12. Workshop better planned	1	1%
13. RUPS was good	* 1	1%
14. RUPS was bad	1	1%
Generalized statement without reference to specifics		
15. Generally good	9	13%

101

Other comments made in varying degrees were about the staff, specific aspects of the workshop, etc. Some of the respondents felt that the experience was good but did not qualify the goodness of the experience or make any comments about how it generalized either to themselves or their jobs, etc. This group constituted 13 percent.

In response to the second question, 99 percent of the people felt that they were more competent to do in-service training, and one person felt that his competence had remained the same (Table 43). No one stated that he had become less competent due to the experience.

TABLE 43

Q 2: Competency to do In-Service Training

		No.	%
A.	More Competent	67	99%
B.	Less Competent	0	-
C.	Remained the Same	1	1%

TABLE 44

Q 3: Plans to use Innovative Technique

		No.	%
A.	Yes	62	91%
B.	None Applicable	1	1%
C.	No	2	3%
	Question not applicable	3	4%

102

The third question (Table 44) brought forth very positive statements from the majority. Ninety-one percent of the respondents felt that they would use innovative techniques in their classrooms (Table 44).

The fourth question (Table 45) dealt with improvement in their skills in attacking problems. There was unanimous agreement that their skills in problem solving had improved.

The fifth question (Table 46) dealt with their reaction to a particular section of the workshop and how meaningful the "RUPS" model was as a learning experience. The majority of

TABLE 45

Q 4: Skills in Problem Solving

		No.	%
A.	Improved	68	100%
B.	Not Improved	0	-
C.	No	0	-

TABLE 46

Q 5: RUPS Model

		No.	%
A.	Very Meaningful	19	28%
B.	Meaningful	39	57%
C.	Somewhat Meaningful	9	13%
D.	Meaningless	1	1%

the participants found the course meaningful. Twenty-eight percent stated that it was "very meaningful," and fifty-seven stated that it was "meaningful." Thirteen percent felt that it was only somewhat meaningful and one person felt that it was "meaningless."

Question 6 (Table 47) dealt with their opinion of whether "RUPS" model should be made available to all teachers in their in-service training. Eighty-five percent of the participants felt that it should be made available and 15 percent had some doubts and could not make up their minds.

Question 7 (Table 48) asked them to describe three aspects of the life-plan program and how it could be adopted in their back-home situations. Twenty-one percent of the respondents did not give any response to this particular aspect. The remaining responses mentioned one and sometimes more than one particular technique. Only one respondent felt that these could not be applied to his/her back-home situation.

TABLE 47

Q 6: Should RUPS Model be made available?

		No.	%
A.	Yes	58	85%
B.	No	0	-
C.	Am Not Sure	10	15%

TABLE 48

Q 7: Description of three aspects of
Life Plan Program that could be
adopted to back home situations.

	No.	%
1. No response	14	21%
2. Life Focus and goals	13	19%
3. Points up common problems	4	6%
4. Helps solve problems	4	6%
5. Helps in understanding student values	10	15%
6. Helps in understanding family, church, or PTA	8	12%
7. Helps in understanding faculty and teachers	13	19%
8. Mention of specific techniques, e.g., life-chart, peak and weak experiences and Jo-Harry window	9	13%
9. Obituary and epitaph	4	6%
10. Feedback	5	7%
11. Partially good	2	3%
12. No help	1	1%

The eighth question (Table 49) asked whether they would recommend the life-plan program (Appendix D) to another group of teachers. The majority of the respondents felt that they would, and a small minority either did not respond or felt that they would not. Ninety-one percent of the respondents felt that they would recommend the life-plan program to other sets of teachers, two people felt that they would not, and 6 percent did not give any opinion at all.

TABLE 49

Q 8: Would you recommend the Life Plan Program?

		No.	%
A.	Yes	62	91%
B.	No	2	3%
	Did Not Answer	4	6%

TABLE 50

Q 9: Usefulness of Dr. X's Talk

		No.	%
A.	Very Useful	11	16%
B.	Useful	27	40%
C.	Slightly Useful	26	38%
D.	Not Useful	3	4%
	Did Not Answer	1	1%

The ninth question dealt with the usefulness of the only lecture given in the workshop. Here the range of opinions was quite varied (Table 50).

The tenth question (Table 51) dealt with the success of the triad T-groups and the degree to which they could make use of the learning opportunities provided in that experience. The majority of participants, namely 62 percent, felt that it was successful and could be applied a great deal.

TABLE 51

Q 10: Success of Triad T-Groups

	No.	%
A. A Great Deal	42	62%
B. Some	25	37%
C. Very Little	1	1%

Question 11 (Table 52) dealt with how their learning opportunities in these triad T-groups could be improved. The responses ranged over a series of topics. Some dealt with their own behavior and others with concrete suggestions.

TABLE 52

Q 11: How learning opportunities could be
improved in the Triad T-Group

	No.	%
1. No response	6	9%
2. By listening better	10	15%
3. By sharing thoughts or by becoming more involved	21	31%
4. By more feedback	8	12%
5. By all participants being from the same county	2	3%
6. By fewer people	1	1%
7. By more exercises	2	3%
8. By more time being spent on it	12	18%
9. By having better trainers or better planning	9	13%
10. No suggestions	7	10%

TABLE 53

Q 12: Involvement and Commitment
to Back Home Plans

	No.	%
A. A Great Deal	44	65%
B. Some	23	34%
C. Very Little	1	1%

108

The twelfth question (Table 53) dealt with their assessment of their involvement and commitment to their back-home plans based on the workshop learning experience. A fairly large majority felt enthusiastic and the remainder somewhat lukewarm, and one person expressed no involvement.

Question 13 (Tables 54 and 55) asked for the most and the least helpful experience in the third week of the workshop concerning "problem solving for back home." The responses

TABLE 54

Q 13a: Experience that was helpful in the
"Problems solving for back home" section

	No.	%
1. No response	7	10%
2. None were helpful	2	3%
3. Force field analysis	16	24%
4. Involving of county personnel	7	10%
5. Problems were brought out and solved	8	12%
6. Getting others involved	2	3%
7. Selecting the problems	3	4%
8. Realizing "things that are necessary"	6	9%
9. T-groups	4	6%
10. Similarity of problems	3	4%
11. Understanding PTA organization	1	1%
12. Feedback	1	1%
13. Commitment to the task	1	1%
14. RUPS	1	1%
15. Building the monument	1	1%
16. Equal participation by all	4	6%
17. Staying in the group and "fighting it out"	1	1%
18. "Going from large perception to small detail"	1	1%

109

ranged over a number of specific details. Ten percent did not respond to the positive aspect of the question, and 46 percent did not specify the least helpful.

The last question (Table 56) asked for any additional comments that the respondents wanted to make. Here 44 percent did not make any comments, while almost an equal number

TABLE 55

Q 13b: Least helpful experience in the
problem solving for back home

	No.	%
1. No response	31	46%
2. Was bored by some	1	1%
3. It was all useful	3	4%
4. Giving consensual answers	2	3%
5. Too much time spent on reporting	5	7%
6. Large group work	1	1%
7. Knowing long range goals that are not soluble	2	3%
8. Writing things that will not be carried out	2	3%
9. Not enough time for triads	20	30%
10. Noise	2	3%
11. Monument	5	7%
12. The last section	1	1%
13. Methods of gaining confidence in people	1	1%
14. Teachers being stubborn	1	1%
15. Lack of discipline	1	1%
16. Brainstorming	1	1%
17. Force theory	1	1%
18. Triads	1	1%
19. Specific behavior of trainers	2	3%

110

made positive statements, and a small minority expressed negative opinions.

TABLE 56

Q 14: Additional comments

	No.	%
1. No response	30	44%
Negative or partially negative comments		
2. Criticism of a trainer	2	3%
3. Too much emphasis on sex	1	1%
4. Too much structure	1	1%
5. Criticism of superintendents and principals	1	1%
6. "We reacted the way it had been planned" (connotation of hidden agenda)	1	1%
7. Useful for others but not me	1	1%
	7	8%
Positive remarks		
8. Hope for personal benefits	12	18%
9. Enjoyable or useful experience	13	19%
10. Best workshop so far	1	1%
11. Helpful for problems of poverty	1	1%
12. Helpful for the county	1	1%
13. Meet new people	1	1%
14. Other teachers should also get it	1	1%
15. More aware of new people	1	1%
	31	43%

In summary, the general response was positive. The majority of the participants were satisfied with the way the workshop was run. There were instances of specific complaints spread over the range of responses. Numerically, they constitute a minority. The data revealed positive reactions to some of the specific techniques used in the workshop.

Interviews

As mentioned above, twenty of the experimental and a sample of twenty matched controls were interviewed at length. Interviews were taped, then transcribed and content analyzed. All interviews were conducted in an open-ended manner. A copy of the guidelines used for the interview is contained in Appendix F.

The interviews brought out a series of developments that had taken place across the state. These changes varied from county to county but did not vary for the two groups. They consisted of such things as changes in jobs within the past two or three years and changes brought about by administrative modifications made in the school system. It was felt that both groups had been exposed to the same sort of changes and that they did not constitute a hardship either in favor of or against a particular group.

Each of the interviews carried an individual flavor. Only a very rough attempt was made to make statistical comparisons. It was felt that descriptive statements would do better justice to the individualistic aspects of the interviews.

A striking difference in the responses of the two groups (experimental and control) to the first question concerning their functioning as a teacher, with very little overlap, was the manner in which the question was interpreted. On the whole, the experimental group perceived this question to refer to intrapersonal changes and talked of changes in their own attitudes, their communication skills, and differences in teaching methods that they had employed.

The control group, on the other hand, generally tended to refer to changes that had taken place in the external environment and talked of changes in their job, changes in the school system, etc.

When the respondents' statements were categorized in

terms of a reference to personal changes as opposed to physical changes, sixteen of the experimental group spontaneously referred to the personal changes and two to the physical changes, whereas five of the controlled referred to personal changes and fourteen to physical changes. The differences are statistically significant at the more than .01 level (of chi-square = 13.80) (Table 57).

TABLE 57

Q 1: Functioning as a Teacher

Nature of Change	Experimental Group	Control Group	Total
Personal Change (including teaching methods)	16	5	21
Physical Change (New job, external circumstances, work load)	2	14	16
Total	18	19	37

x^2 = 13.80; p < .001

A look at the types of responses will give a flavor of the differences in the groups. The following are some of the comments:

"The discipline in my room has changed radically. Formerly, I would paddle any child who answered me in a sarcastic manner. Now I look for the why, the reason the child is misbehaving. I tell my students that they may express their opinions, but they must express them in an acceptable manner."

"I feel more comfortable. I have better relations with teachers. I know the difference between respect and fear of authority, and I feel more open."

"I have learned to speak out more. I feel more 'in the group

113

with the others.' I feel more a participant and less an observer."

"I feel more receptive to others' suggestions and complaints."

"I look at other person's side of problems more," or "I am accepting people even when I can't accept ideas," or "I feel more aware of feelings of others."

"I have realized a limitation within myself. That is, I am not emotionally geared for working with special types of children."

"I place greater emphasis on involving the whole group."

"I permit class discussions to stray from subject matter occasionally."

Some of the participants had tried to apply procedures they had learned in the training labs. Some of them said, for instance, that they had tried role playing in their classes or that they had allowed subordinate teachers to share responsibility of presiding over faculty meetings. One of the principals stated that he liked to find out why a student is indifferent and used this information in compiling tests in order to get these students actively involved.

Generally speaking, the experimental group was clearly aware of their interpersonal relationships and felt that they had changed and that their function as a teacher was due to the change within themselves rather than to other changes. This is not to say that they were not aware at all of the physical changes that were also mentioned. However, as stated above, the predominance of the topics mentioned referred to the interpersonal relationships with emphasis on the change having been brought about because of intrapersonal changes.

As opposed to this, the control group was not that preoccupied with or that aware of their own role. With the exception of five people who referred to their personal involvement sometimes in positive and sometimes in negative ways, the majority of the group referred to the changes that had taken place in the total school structure. Some of the following were typical:

"I have a new job; it's a different type of a job."

"The curriculum is more strenuous, and I have felt it necessary to teach several classes, which makes me feel not completely involved in any job."

"This is my first year at a new type of school, and I am teaching more academic subjects than I used to."

"We are now trying out a new method, the phonetic method, and I feel that I am not covering as much material as in previous years."

Some in the group expressed a sense of frustration in coping with problems raised by heavier teaching load, larger classes, scarce equipment, and overcrowding in schools.

A few of the control group referred to changes within themselves. Some of these statements were positive. For example, one respondent said that he felt more confident in himself, he had better insight, and, overall, he had learned to cope better, though he could not pinpoint the reasons. Another respondent said that she felt "more relaxed in the classroom. I talk more to my students to discover their problems." A third one stated that he saw his role as a superintendent differently. He felt that he represented the teachers and the students more and the board of education less. A few of them were dissatisfied with what was happening. One of them felt strongly, that her work had deteriorated compared to other years, and another one was concerned about "dispelling my image as an angry and sour teacher. I am trying to control my temper more."

Since there is no reason to assume that the experimental group had fewer problems to face in their jobs, it is interesting to see the differences between the two groups. The experimental group was very much aware of changes within themselves and felt that these led to some changes in the environment. They saw their function as a teacher changed not because of the external changes but because of the change that they had experienced within themselves. They, therefore, became a source of change themselves.

The second question became a little more specific and asked if they had done anything differently as a teacher in the school year (or in the past two years), as compared to prior years. At a general level, we find that both the groups did things differently. It seems that there had been changes in their functions.

Only one of the experimental group and only three out of the control stated that there had been no change. These differences, in terms of change or no change across the two groups, are not statistically significant (Table 58).

TABLE 58

Q 2: "Done differently" as a Teacher

	Experimental Group	Control Group	Total
Yes	17	16	33
No	1	3	4
Total	18	19	37

$x^2 = 1.80$; $p < .50$

An examination of the answers revealed a persistence of the earlier theme, that is, the experimental group tended more to talk about interpersonal relationships and how they could modify these, as opposed to the control group, which, to some extent, tended more to concentrate on changes residing outside themselves. There is a certain degree of overlap here, but the dominant themes still seem to be different. One teacher reported an instance of a change in attitude toward discipline. He said that a child who had stolen five dollars was told by him that if the child returned the money he would not be paddled, something that he would not have done in previous years. Another respondent mentioned the case of a student who she felt was not performing up to par. The teacher went out of the way to talk to the girl and to do things for her to show her that she was wanted and was liked. In both instances, the respondents felt that they would not have been conscious of seeking alternate ways of handling children's problems.

Other members of the experimental group stated that they took special interest in problem students, that they asked students how students feel about things, that they went out of their way to communicate with those that they dealt with, and tried to get all rather than a few involved in the activities. They felt that they were more expressive, that they had allowed the students to join in planning their classes, that they had let the students express themselves more, that they had asked the parents to encourage them, that they had listened more to find out what the students liked and how they felt about the instructor. One of the respondents said that she was jotting down ideas about how to help teachers have a better classroom experience. She added that she felt that she now confronted problems rather than avoided them and that she offered her own ideas with less anxiety than she used to.

In sharp contrast to the experimental group, the control group mentioned such things as use of new workbooks in the courses, or, "I let students work more on their own and give longer lectures. Both of these changes are due to the fact that the students I am working with this year are more mature than those of last year." A third one said that she is working with the whole class and then dividing them into small groups or that she was very involved with the new phonetic techniques being used. One person mentioned that he was handling students differently and was being more sympathetic toward the students as individuals. Some mentioned a change of subject matter or the type of work that they used. One person had sent a survey to parents concerning children's reaction to the kindergarten to better understand the school or that they had worked especially hard to change some of the programs. Generally speaking, it seems that the control-group teacher does not see himself as the change agent as much as the experimental group does.

The next question (Question 3) referred to the respondent's relationship with other teachers or colleagues. Here again, we get rather striking differences in the two groups.

The experimental group talked in terms of greater awareness of others, of better communication with others, of greater acceptance of others, and of being more open to others. None of them felt that there had been any negative interaction with other teachers or colleagues. In contrast to this, the control group predominantly (fourteen out of nineteen) stated that there had been no change in their relationships with their colleagues. Three of the controls had some negative statements about their relationships, and one had some positive statements. Categorizing the responses in terms of positive, negative, or no change, the two groups show a statistically significant difference (chi-square 31.20 significant beyond the .001 level) (Table 59).

TABLE 59

Q 3: Related Differently to Other Teachers or Peers

	Experimental Group	Control Group	Total
Changed in a positive manner	17	1	18
Changed in a negative manner	0	3	3
No change	0	14	3
No reply	1	1	2
Total	18	19	37

x^2 = 31.20; p < .001

A look at the type of responses given by the two groups shows that the experimental group tended to talk about such things as, "I'm more conscious of the complexity of things," "I place greater emphasis in working together and therefore am more cooperative," "I try to see how others feel," "I try to hear the problems more," "I'm more sensitive to others' problems," "I'm more aware of teachers' feelings and talents through communication," "Association with other teachers has helped me more than anything else," "I do less prejudging of a problem and am more accepting of a problem," "I feel more a part and they seem closer to me. I feel I can talk to them more," "I do not feel as shy and speak out more in interrelationships," "I make a conscious effort to be tolerant of others' views if they are different from mine."

The control group, on the other hand, predominantly felt that there had been no change in their relationships. It seemed that the control group reported no changes with implications of that connoting steadfastness and loyalty. One person mentioned that the change had been in a positive direction. She stated that she now had more meaningful relationships with the other teachers. This respondent attributed this change to an in-service program. The three negative responses consisted of such things as the respondent's feeling that the other teachers were not working as hard as she was or that there was not as much "cooperation as there used to be," or "there is less contact between the teachers than there used to be."

Question 4 specifically asked about any change in activities within these relationships with other teachers or peers. A look at Table 60 indicates that twelve, that is a majority of the experimental group, felt that the change had been of a positive nature. None of the control group felt that the activities had changed in a positive direction. One each in both the groups felt that the change had been in a negative direction, and one out of the experimental and three out of the control felt that the changes could be attributed to new jobs. Statistically speaking, the differences between the two groups are significant at the .01 level (chi-square 19.21).

Some of the responses given by the experimental group

TABLE 60

Q 4: Activities Differed in Relation to Teachers or Peers

	Experimental Group	Control Group	Total
Changed in a positive direction	12	0	12
Changed in a negative direction	0	2	2
No change	5	10	15
New job	0	3	4
No response	1	4	5
Total	18	19	37

$x^2 = 19.21$; $p < .001$

reveal reference to better communication, better involvement with others in similar activities, better participation, etc. Some of the examples of types of responses in this connection were, "I gave advice to a new teacher upon request, which I would not have done before," or "I gave a program on sensitivity training that got the teachers involved," or "tried unsuccessfully to start a sensitivity training group but am trying to change meetings to make them more interesting and am trying to gain more political power for the teachers." Some others stated that they were trying to encourage teachers to participate actively in faculty meetings by allowing them to share the task of presiding over meetings. Some others still felt that they were trying to work as a team on similar problems or "work more closely with peers."

Three out of the control group felt that there had been negative change. Their responses consisted of such things as "I don't associate with the teachers because they are catty," or "There is a lack of trust and not as much interaction as there used to be. I do not feel at ease," or "Relationships have gotten bad because of the political split." Three of the control group felt that new jobs had brought about changes that had led to different types of activities with their peers. They mentioned changes in the structure of their roles that had led to more or less contact with the peers.

The next two questions dealt with the respondents' relationships with their superiors and any particular kinds of activities that had changed in this context. Question 5 dealt with

TABLE 61

Q 5: Relation with Superiors

	Experimental Group	Control Group	Total
Changed in a positive direction	11	9	20
Changed in a negative direction	1	3	4
No change	5	6	11
New job	1	1	1
Total	18	19	37

$x^2 = 4.08$; $p < .30$

121

their relationship with their superiors and Question 6 with their particular activities. The group differences are not so pronounced in these cases as they had been in the categories dealt above. The groups did not show any particular change in their relationships with their superiors (Tables 61 and 62).

TABLE 62

Q 6: Activities in Relationship with Superiors

	Experimental Group	Control Group	Total
Changed in a positive direction	8	3	11
Changed in a negative direction	0	3	3
Changed in job structure hence no comparison possible	2	5	7
Change in attitude (positive)	4	1	5
No change	4	7	11
Total	18	19	37

$x^2 = 9.18$; $p < .10$

It may be interesting to see the manner in which the two groups talk about the positive relationship with their superiors. The experimentals mentioned better communication with their superiors. Some of the respondents stated that they felt freer to express their opinion; they felt less inferior and felt more confident in their relationships. Some felt that they had been of more help to their principal or felt closer to the principal, especially the ones who had had sensitivity training.

The control group mentioned more contact with the superintendent either because of a new job or because of the political situation within the board of education. Some of the negative comments made by the group were that they felt that in one case the superior had neglected the job because of political differences and another that the size of the faculty of the school had made it harder to see the principal.

Question 7 dealt with relationships with the students, or their subordinates if the respondent happened to be a principal or a board member. In this case, the differences between the groups were not marked and did not approach statistical significance (Table 63).

TABLE 63

Q 7: Relationship with Students or Subordinates

	Experimental Group	Control Group	Total
Changed in a positive direction	15	11	26
Changed in a negative direction	0	2	2
No change	2	6	8
No response	1	0	1
Total	18	19	37

$x^2 = 5.65$; $p < .20$

Question 8 dealt with change in activities related to students. The chief source of difference between the groups appears to be self-initiated activities, that is, activities that were instituted by the teacher or the superior in question (Table 64). Some of the members of the experimental group mentioned that they let the students take part in planning and sought to find out the students' interests. One or two of the respondents described specific incidents in which they had tried to use special games that the students could use in classwork in order to get them more involved. Some felt that they were now more realistic in their dealings with problem children and that they could encourage their subordinates to work toward their problems more adequately than they used to.

The small number of the control group who mentioned particular activities that they had instituted explained that these took the form of greater emphasis on participation and less on tests or giving students more work to do. A greater number of the control mentioned change in the job or changes in the school as the impetus for the difference. These were regarded as externally instituted changes. The differences between these two groups along these dimensions are statistically significant at greater than .01 level (chi-square = 10.14) (Table 64).

The last two questions, Questions 9 and 10, dealt with the participants' relationships with their communities. Seven out of the experimental and three out of the control did not refer to any community relationships. The remainder of the respondents regarded the relationships to be better, worse, or not changed. The group differences in this category are significant statistically at more than .05 level (Table 65).

The experimental group generally felt that they had joined many more groups, were more active, had better relationships with the PTA, or that they had actively tried to interact with people.

The control-group respondents mentioned spending more time working for the PTA or the churches. A few felt that they were doing less in the community than they used to or that the

TABLE 64

Q 8: Activities in Dealing with Subordinates

	Experimental Group	Control Group	Total
Self-initiated changes	13	4	17
Externally initiated changes	3	7	10
No change	2	8	10
Total	18	19	37

$x^2 = 10.14$; $p < .01$

TABLE 65

Q 9: Relationships with the Community

	Experimental Group	Control Group	Total
Better relationships	7	3	10
Worse relationships	0	3	3
No change	4	10	14
No response	7	3	10
Total	18	19	37

$x^2 = 8.78$; $p < .05$

community had enlarged, which made active participation difficult.

The last question, number 10, dealt with the activities within the community that had been different. The differences between the two groups were not statistically significant (Table 66).

TABLE 66

Q 10: Activities with Relationship to Community

	Experimental Group	Control Group	Total
More activities	11	4	15
Fewer activities	2	3	5
No change	4	10	14
No response	1	2	3
Total	18	19	37

$x^2 = 6.48$; $p < .10$

The experimental group mentioned such things as visiting the community and taking more part in the local politics. None of them felt that they were doing poorly.

One of the probes used by some of the interviewers attempted to gauge the intrapersonal change felt by the respondents in the past two or three years, the three years being the period when the experimental group had been involved in sensitivity training. No quantitative analysis was made of this answer, but it seems that a great majority of the experimental group felt that the greatest amount of change within them had come due to the sensitivity training. Some of them mentioned other events in their life, but at least half of them felt that the greatest amount of change had occurred during these past three years. The control group, on the other hand, mentioned several events in the course of their life not concentrated in the same period of time. They mentioned such events as a new academic course, sickness, experiences in the army, a death in the family, or that they had been told some unpleasant things by others around them.

A review of the transcripts of the interviews indicated a difference in the language used by the two groups. The experimental group tended to talk about more participation, more acceptance, more involvement, more problem solving, and the control group talked more on a level of how they could relate to other people. It seemed that the experimental group had acquired a new set of concepts that they used in their classroom situations. To what extent the language communicated and conveyed the specific nature of the activities and to what extent these activities were, in fact, different is difficult to judge.

In summary, then, it appears that the two groups did react differentially and did perceive the changes within themselves as being different. An overall impression is of almost an acquisition of a new "culture" by the experimental group. This culture constituted attention to communication, mutual acceptance, greater participation, problem solving, etc. The control group apparently had not acquired such a vocabulary and tended to express generally more negative attitudes. There was a predominance of positive phrases used by the experimental group. It almost seems that the experimental group did not concentrate on the problems that must arise in their daily living and did not seem as aware of the obstacles that they faced. The experimental group tended to feel that they had changed and therefore had a different approach to the same problems, whereas the control group tended to ascribe changes to external sources.

Chapter VI

SUMMARY

The assessment described in the previous pages involved a somewhat unique undertaking. A group of educators from a region, described generally as "depressed and backward," spent a few weeks of their summers undergoing sensitivity training for three years. In addition, an attempt was made to measure the effects of this experience and compare the changes with those of a control group of educators who had not been exposed to such training. It may be assumed that since the experimental group was recommended by their superiors, they represented those that would have gained most from the experience. However, a pretesting during the second year of the program showed no differences between the two groups.

In the first year, the educators spent two weeks undergoing sensitivity training in a central location and met subsequently on a weekly basis. No systematic assessment was undertaken.

In the second year, 150 participants went through a similar experience. At this time, a comprehensive assessment program was instituted. Measures derived from such different theoretical models of personality as Leary, Cattel, Shoestrom, and Frankel-Brunswik were used. They were pretested prior to the training, post-tested right after the three-week training period, and again six months later. A control group of fifty went through the pretest and the second post-test procedures.

128

In summary, the results of the extensive assessment program demonstrated that the participants had changed and that the change had occurred in different directions and at different times. The assessment program also attempted to see if those who came in contact with these participants, namely, their superiors and their students, perceived them differently. Here again, some differences were found.

During the third year of the program, only seventy-five participants were involved in another series of sensitivity training techniques. At this time, no large-scale assessment was attempted since it would have essentially been a duplication of the assessment done in the second year. These participants, however, gave subjective reactions to the training program at the end of the three weeks. Approximately six months later, twenty of these participants (experimental group) were followed up in interviews. A group of twenty other educators and educational administrators (control group) were also interviewed in order to make comparisons.

As the preceding pages have reported, the participants changed in varied and significant ways compared to the control group. Previous studies concerned with changes due to sensitivity training (Bennis, Burke, Cutter, Herrington, and Hoffman, 1957; Burke and Bennis, 1961) had not used a control group.

The extensive assessment program demonstrated that the educators became less authoritarian, less rigid, and more open-minded. They became more time competent, that is, they were able to tie the past and the future to the present in a meaningful continuity. They developed greater faith in the future without rigid or overly realistic goals. It also seems that the educators' ability to use good judgment in the application of values increased. They became more sensitive to their own needs and feelings. They accepted their own weaknesses and increased their capacity for intimate contact. They became less distrustful of others and saw themselves as, forceful leaders. Not surprisingly, in view of these developments, their self-concept improved.

These changes, along with others too numerous to be recapitulated here, were accompanied by some differences in the perception of the two groups by those that were most affected by them, namely, their superiors and their students. The supervisors viewed the experimental group more positively than the control group. The students who had come in contact with the two groups of educators at an overt level painted a rather negative picture of the teachers and in sharp contrast to the teachers self-perception. However, at a more covert level, the interactions had brought forth very striking differences. It was apparent that if a student had interacted with a teacher who had been through the sensitivity training, he was more likely to project such activities as learning, studying, preparing for the future, feel a sense of identity with the teacher whose punishing activities he perceived as being for his own good, seeing the future optimistically and himself as a source of effective action than if he got a teacher who had not had such training.

The interview analysis demonstrated that experimental and control groups reacted differently. The great majority of the experimental group members felt that the greatest amount of change within themselves had come due to the sensitivity training. The controls mentioned several events in the course of their lives extended over a wider time period.

A most striking difference was the perception of the problems with the experimental group, utilizing insights and language of the sensitivity training experience and thus emphasizing complexity and psychological dimensions compared to the control group. These changes extended to all the significant job-related relationships of the educators.

The assessment program had its share of handicaps and shortcomings chiefly due to ongoing budgetary cuts. The statistical analysis varied from being extensive to more descriptive with the economic vicissitudes.

The major neglected area in the study was the role of the trainers. Each set of trainers set up a different type of a training program, depending on his or her theoretical allegiance as well as value systems. The program, therefore, evolved as a function of what the trainers regarded as the most useful experience of the teachers. One would assume that these judgments were based on the trainers' prior experiences with the types of groups that they had dealt with.

It would be interesting to see what role the trainers played in this enterprise, the effects that the trainers' personality value systems and goals had on the participants. In short, the trainers should also be measured along the dimensions used to assess the participants.

Appendix A

ICL SUBSCALES

1. *Managerial-Autocratic (AP)*: a person scoring high on the subscale is dictatorial and expects everyone to admire him. He manages others and is bossy. He tries to be too successful and always gives advice to others. A person scoring low on this scale likes responsibility, is a good leader, and is forceful. He is able to give orders, makes a good impression, and is often admired and respected by others. He is well thought of.

2. *Competitive-Narcissistic (BC)*: a person scoring high on this subscale is cold and unfeeling, egotistical and conceited. He is shrewd and calculating and thinks only of himself. He is somewhat snobbish, proud and self-satisfied, and boastful. A person scoring low on this subscale can be indifferent to others. He is self-reliant, assertive, self-confident, independent, and businesslike. He likes to compete with others. He is able to take care of himself and is also self-respecting.

3. *Aggressive-Sadistic (DE)*: a person scoring high on this subscale is hard-hearted, cruel, and unkind. He is often unfriendly, frequently angry, and outspoken. He is impatient with others' mistakes. He is self-seeking and sarcastic. A person scoring low on this subscale is straightforward and direct. He is critical of others and irritable. He is hard-boiled when necessary, stern but fair, and firm but just. He can be frank and honest and can be strict if necessary.

4. *Rebellious-Distrustful (FG)*: a person scoring high on this subscale is rebellious against everything and distrusts everybody. He is bitter, resentful, and complaining. He is jealous, stubborn, and slow to forgive a wrong. A person scoring low on this subscale is skeptical, often gloomy, and resents being bossed. He is hard to impress, touchy and easily hurt, and frequently disappointed. He can complain if necessary and is able to doubt others.

5. *Self-effacing-Masochistic (HI)*: a person scoring high on this subscale is always ashamed of himself. He is shy, timid, and self-punishing. He is spineless, meek, passive and unaggressive, and obeys too willingly. A person scoring low on this subscale is modest, easily led, and usually gives in. He is able to criticize himself and can be obedient.

6. *Docile-Dependent (JK)*: a person scoring high on this subscale is a clinging vine and will believe anyone. He is dependent, wants to be led, and hardly ever talks back. He is easily fooled. He likes to be taken care of and lets others make decisions. A person scoring low on this subscale is often helped by others, admires and imitates others, and is very respectful to authority. He accepts advice readily, is trusting and eager to please, and very anxious to be approved of. He is grateful and appreciative.

7. *Cooperative-over-Conventional (LM)*: a person scoring high on this subscale agrees with everyone and loves everyone. He will confide in anyone, is too easily influenced by his friends, and wants everyone's love. He likes everybody and is friendly all the time. A person scoring low on this subscale is warm, sociable, and neighborly. He is affectionate and understanding and wants everyone to like him. He is always pleasant and agreeable and eager to get along with others. He is cooperative and friendly.

8. *Responsible-Hypernormal (NO)*: a person scoring high on this subscale tries to comfort everyone. He spoils people with kindness, is too willing to give to others, is overprotective of others, and is generous to a fault. He is oversympathetic, forgives anything, and is too lenient with others. A person scoring low on this subscale enjoys taking care of others. He is kind, reassuring, tender, and softhearted. He gives freely of himself and encourages others. He is helpful and considerate.

Appendix B

POI—SUBSCALES

Number of Items	Scale Number	Symbol	Description
I. Ratio Scores			
23	½	TıTc	TIME RATIO Time incompetence Time competence—measures degree to which one is "present" oriented
127	¾	O/I	SUPPORT RATIO Other/inner—measures whether reactivity orientation is basically toward others or self
II. Subscales			
26	5	SAV	SELF-ACTUALIZING VALUE Measures affirmation of a primary value of self-actualizing people
32	6	Ex	EXISTENTIALITY Measures ability to situationally or existentially react without rigid adherence to principles
23	7	Fr	FEELING REACTIVITY Measures sensitiviy of responsiveness to one's own needs and feelings
18	8	S	SPONTANEITY Measures freedom to react spontaneously or to be oneself

16	9	Sr	SELF-REGARD
			Measures affirmation of self because of worth or strength
26	10	Sa	SELF-ACCEPTANCE
			Measures affirmation or acceptance of self in spite of weaknesses or deficiencies
16	11	Nc	NATURE OF MAN
			Measures degree of the constructive view of the nature of man, masculinity, femininity
9	12	Sy	SYNERGY
			Measures ability to be synergistic, to transcend dichotomies
25	13	A	ACCEPTANCE OF AGGRESSION
			Measures ability to accept one's natural aggressiveness as opposed to defensiveness, denial, and repression of aggression
28	14	C	CAPACITY FOR INTIMATE CONTACT
			Measures ability to develop contactful intimate relationships with other human beings, unencumbered by expectations and obligations

Appendix C

THE TEN DYNAMIC STRUCTURES MEASURED IN MAT

	Title	Symbol on the Records	Brief Description
ERGS (Drives)	Mating Erg	(Ma)	Strength of the normal, heterosexual, or mating drive.
	Assertiveness Erg	(As)	Strength of the drive of self-assertion, mastery, and achievement.
	Fear (Escape) Erg	(Fr)	Level of alertness to external dangers (This is not anxiety; see [34] and p. 22)
	Narcissism-comfort Erg	(Na)	Level of drive to sensuous, indulgent satisfactions.
	Pugnacity-sadism Erg	(Pg)	Strength of destructive, hostile impulses.
SENTI-MENTS	Self-concept sentiment	(SS)	Level of concern about the self-concept, social repute, and more remote rewards.
	Superego sentiment	(SE)	Strength of development of conscience.

Career sentiment	(Ca)	Amount of development of interests in a career.
Sweetheart-spouse sentiment	(Sw)	Strength of attachment to wife (husband or sweetheart).
Home-parental sentiment	(Ho)	Strength of attitudes attaching to the parental home.

Appendix D

SECOND WEEK PROGRAM OF THE THIRD-YEAR PARTICIPANTS

1. Life line
2. Discuss
3. Ten descriptions of self, "Who Am I?"
4. Priority arrangement
5. Discuss
6. Obituary and epitaph
7. Discuss
8. Who would I like to be?
9. A day or two in your life ten years from now
10. Eight (8) categories—listed below
11. Formulate projects to get to do things well you want to do well

Categories

1. Peak experiences (a list of things that matter to you)
2. Things I do well
3. Things I do poorly
4. Things I would like to stop doing
5. Things I would like to learn to do well
6. Peak experiences I would like to have
7. Values to be realized
8. Things I would like to start doing now

Appendix E

FEEDBACK QUESTIONNAIRE

We are very interested in learning about your reactions to the three weeks' workshop. We will greatly appreciate your honest and frank answers to the following questions. We do not want you to give your name.

1. Did the workshop meet your expectation? Yes   No

   a) If yes, in what ways?

   b) If no, why not?

2. Please check one of the following:

   a) I feel that this experience has made me more competent to do in-service training in the back-home situation.
   b) I feel that this experience has made me less competent to do in-service training in the back-home situation.
   c) My competency for in-service training has remained the same.

3. Please check one of the following: As a result of this experience:

   a) I plan to use innovative techniques in my classroom.
   b) I feel that none of these techniques are applicable in the classroom.
   c) I do not plan to use any of these techniques in my classroom.

4. Do you feel that as a result of this experience:

   a) Your skills in problem solving have improved.
   b) Your skills in problem solving have not improved.
   c) Your skills in problem solving are the same.

5. How meaningful was the RUPS model to you as a learning experience?

   a) Very meaningful
   b) Meaningful
   c) Somewhat meaningful
   d) Meaningless

6. Do you feel that the RUPS model should be made available to all teachers in their in-service training program?
   Yes   No   Am not sure

7. Briefly describe how you could adapt three aspects of the Life Plan Program to back home situations.

8. Would you recommend the Life Plan Program to another group of teachers? Yes   No

9. How useful did you find the talk of Dr. Busby?

   a) Very useful
   b) Useful
   c) Slightly useful
   d) Not useful

10. How would you rate the degree of success you had in making use of the learning opportunities provided in the triad (three concentric circles) T-groups?

   a) A great deal
   b) Some
   c) Very little

11. How could your learning opportunities in the Triad T group be improved?

12. How would you rate your involvement and commitment to your back-home plans from this learning experience?

   a) A great deal
   b) Some
   c) Very little

13a. What experience in the "problem solving for back home" helped you the most?

13b. What experience in the "problem solving for back home" helped you the least?

14. Any other comments?

Appendix F

QUESTIONS USED AS GUIDELINES FOR INTERVIEWS

NAME:

1. How do you feel you have functioned as a teacher in this school year so far as compared to previous years?

2. Have you done anything differently as a teacher in this school year as compared to other years?

3. Do you feel that you have related differently to other teachers in this school year as compared to previous years?

4. Have your activities as related to other teachers been any different during this school year as compared to previous years?

5. Do you feel that you have related differently to your superiors (e.g., principal) during this school year as compared to previous years?

6. Do you think that your role has been different during this school year in school activities that involve you and your superiors (e.g., principal) as compared to previous school years?

7. Do you feel that you have related differently to students during this school year as compared to previous years?

8. Have your activities as related to students been any different during this school year as compared to previous years?

9. Do you feel that you have related differently to your community (e.g., PTA groups, etc.) during this school year as compared to previous years?

10. Have your activities as related to your community (e.g., PTA groups, etc.) been any different during this school year as compared to previous years?

REFERENCES

Adorno, T. W.; Brunswik-Frenkel, Else; Levinson, Daniel J.; and Sanford, Nevitt. *The Authoritarian Personality*. New York: Harper and Row, 1950.

Anderson, H. H., and Brewer, H. M. Studies of teacher classroom personalities. American Psychological Association. *Applied Psychology Monograph* (1945): 6, 157.

Andrew, G.; Hartwell, S. W.; Hutt, M. L.; and Walton, R. E. *The Michigan Picture Test*. Chicago: Science Research Associates, Inc. 1953.

Argyris, C. *Interpersonal Competence and Organization Behavior*. Homewood, Illinois: Dorsey Press, 1962.

Barr, A. S. The measurement of teaching ability. *Journal of Educational Research*. 28 (1935): 561–569.

Bellott, F. K. Design for Tennessee Assessment and Evaluation of Title III ESEA. Memphis State University, College of Education, Bureau of Education Research and Services, Memphis, Tennessee, 1969.

Bennis, W.; Burke, R.; Cutter, H.; Harrington, H.; and Hoffman, J. A note on some problems of measurement and prediction in a training group. *Group Psychotherapy* 10 (1957): 326–341.

Birnbaum, M. Sense and nonsense about sensitivity training. *Saturday Review*, November 1969, pp. 82–83.

Bradford, L. The teaching-learning transaction. *Adult Education* 8 (1958): 135–145.

Bradford, L. P.; Gibb, J. R.; and Benne, K. D. *T group theory and laboratory method*. New York: John Wiley and Sons, 1964.

Burke, H. L., and Bennis, W. G. Changes in perception of self and others during human relations training. *Human Relations* 14 (1961): 165–182.

Bush, R. N. *The Teacher-Pupil Relationship*. Englewood Cliffs, N.J.: Prentice-Hall, 1954.

Campbell, J. P., and Dunnette, M. D. Effectiveness of T-group experiences in managerial training and development. *Psychological Bulletin*, 70 (1968) 73–104.

Cattell, R. B. *Personality: A Systematic Theoretical and Factual Study.* New York: McGraw-Hill, 1950.

Cattell, R. B.; Horn, J. L.; Sweeny, A. B.; and Radcliffe, J. *Motivation Analysis Test.* Champaign, Ill.: Institute for Personality and Ability Testing, 1964.

Cogan, M. L. The behavior of teachers and the productive behavior of their pupils. *Journal of Experimental Education* 27 (1958): 89–124.

Combs, A. *The Professional Education of Teachers.* Boston: Allyn and Bacon, 1965.

Flanders, N. A. Teacher influence, pupil attitudes, and achievement. Washington, D.C.: U. S. Printing Office, 1965, *Cooperative Research Monograph*, No. 12.

Getzels, J. W., and Jackson, P. W. The teacher's personality and characteristics. In N. L. Gage (ed.): *Handbook of Research on Teaching.* Chicago: Rand McNally and Co., 1963, pp. 506–583.

Guilford, J. P. *Fundamental Statistics in Psychology and Education.* New York: McGraw-Hill, 1965.

Gump, P. V. Environmental guidance of the classroom behavioral system. In B. J. Biddle and W. J. Ellena (eds.): *Contemporary Research on Teacher Effectiveness.* New York: Holt, Rinehart, and Winston, Inc., 1964, 165–195.

Jung, C., and Lippitt, R. Utilization of scientific knowledge for change in education. *Theory into Practice.* Portland, Ore.: Research Utilizing Problem Solving, 1966.

Knowles, E. S. A bibliography of research since 1960. *Explorations: Human relations training and research.* Washington, D.C.: NEA, 1967.

Leary, T. *Interpersonal Diagnosis of Personality.* New York: Ronald Press, 1956.

Leary, T. (with collaboration of Helen Lane, Anne Apfelbaum, Mary Della Ciopp, and Charlotte Kaufman). *Multilevel Measurement of Interpersonal Behavior.* Berkeley, Calif.: Psychological Consultation Service, 1956.

Martin, H. O. The assessment of training. *Personnel Management* 39 (1957): 88–93.

Maslow, A., *Towards a Psychology of Being.* New York: Van Nostrand, 1962.

Maslow, A. Huminatas. Institute of Man, Duquesue University, Pittsburgh, Pa., 1967. In R. Knapp, *The Measurement of Self-actualization and its Theoretical Implications.* California Educational Testing Service, 1971.

146

Mathis, A. G. "Development and Validation of a Trainability Index for Laboratory Training Groups." Unpublished doctoral dissertation, University of Chicago, 1955.

Moustakas, C. E. *The Teacher and the Child*. New York: McGraw-Hill, Inc., 1956.

Murray, H. A. *Thematic Apperception Test*. Cambridge: Harvard University Press, 1943.

Odiorne, G. The trouble with sensitivity training. *Journal of American Society of Training Directors* 17 (1963): 9–20.

Osgood, C.; Suci, George J. and Tannenbaum, Percy H. *The Measurement of Meaning*. Urbana: University of Illinois Press, 1957.

Prescott, D. A. *Emotions and Educative Process*. Washington, D.C.: American Council on Education, 1938.

Rogers, C. R. A plan for self-directed change in an educational system. *Educational Leadership* 24 (1967): 717–731.

Rotter, J. B. *Social Learning and Clinical Psychology*. Englewood Cliffs, N.J.: Prentice-Hall, 1954.

Rotter, J. B. Generalized expectancies for internal versus external control of reinforcement. *Psychological Monographs*, 80 (1966).

Ryan, D. G. *Characteristics of Teachers*. Washington, D.C.: American Council of Education, 1960.

Shostrom, E. *Personal Orientation Inventory*. San Diego: Educational and Industrial Testing Service, 1966.

Siegel, S. *Non-Parametric Statistics for the Behavioral Sciences*. New York: McGraw-Hill, 1956.

Snedecor, G. *Statistical Methods Applied to Experiments in Agriculture and Biology*. Ames: Iowa State College Press, 1962.

State of Tennessee Department of Education, Annual Statistical Report, Nashville, Tennessee, Tennessee State Department of Education, 1958, 1965.

Thurstone, L. L., *Primary Mental Abilities*. Psychometric Monograph, No. 1; lx.

Thurstone, L. L., "Factor Analysis as a Scientific Method with Special Reference to the Analysis of Human Traits," in Wirth L. (1940), *Eleven Twenty Six, a Decade of Social Science Research*. Chicago: University of Chicago Press, pp. 78–112.

Thurstone, L. L., *Multiple Factor Analysis*. Chicago: University of Chicago Press, 1947.

Wedell, C. C. "A Study of Measurement in Group Dynamics Laboratories." Unpublished doctoral dissertation, George Washington University, 1957.

Weller, Jack E. *Yesterday's People: Life in Contemporary Appalachia*. Lexington: University of Kentucky Press, 1966.

Winer, B. J., *Statistical Principles in Experimental Design*. New York: McGraw-Hill, 1962.